NEW SELECTED POEMS

1988–2013

SEAMUS HEANEY

New Selected Poems

1988–2013

FABER & FABER

First published in 2014
by Faber & Faber Ltd
Bloomsbury House
74–77 Great Russell Street
London WCIB 3DA

Typeset by Faber & Faber Ltd
Printed and bound by
GGP Media GmbH, Pößneck, Germany

A CIP record for this book
is available from the British Library

ISBN 978–0–571–32171–1

2 4 6 8 10 9 7 5 3 1

Publisher's Note

This edition reproduces selections from *Seeing Things* (1991) and *The Spirit Level* (1996) that Seamus Heaney made for *Opened Ground: Poems 1966–1996*. Selections from *Electric Light* (2001), *District and Circle* (2006) and *Human Chain* (2010) were prepared by the author for a prospective edition of his works in Italian translation. Although Seamus Heaney had not identified an extract from *Beowulf* (1999), he did indicate that he would wish to see it represented in that edition, and had previously chosen passages from the opening and closing sections included here. 'In Time', Seamus Heaney's last poem, appears here in accordance with the wishes of his family.

*The Heaney family would like to extend their gratitude
to Marco Sonzogni for his help in producing this edition*

Contents

[vii]

[ix]

NEW SELECTED POEMS

1988–2013

The Golden Bough

from Virgil, Aeneid, VI

Aeneas was praying and holding on to the altar
When the prophetess started to speak: 'Blood relation of
  gods,
Trojan, son of Anchises, the way down to Avernus is easy.
Day and night black Pluto's door stands open.
But to retrace your steps and get back to upper air,
This is the real task and the real undertaking.
A few have been able to do it, sons of the gods
Favoured by Jupiter Justus, or exalted to heaven
In a blaze of heroic glory. Forests spread half-way down
And Cocytus winds through the dark, licking its banks.
Still, if love torments you so much and you so much desire
To sail the Stygian lake twice and twice to inspect
The underworld dark, if you must go beyond what's
  permitted,
Understand what you must do beforehand.
Hidden in the thick of a tree is a bough made of gold
And its leaves and pliable twigs are made of it too.
It is sacred to underworld Juno, who is its patron,
And overtopped by a grove where deep shadows mass
Along far wooded valleys. No one is ever permitted
To go down into earth's hidden places unless he has first
Plucked this golden-fledged tree-branch out of its tree
And bestowed it on fair Proserpina, to whom it belongs
By decree, her own special gift. And when it is plucked
A second one grows in its place, golden once more,
And the foliage growing upon it glimmers the same.
Therefore look up and search deep and when you have
  found it

Take hold of it boldly and duly. If fate has called you
The bough will come away easily, of its own sweet
    accord.
Otherwise, no matter how much strength you muster,
    you won't
Ever manage to quell it or fell it with the toughest
    of blades.'

Markings

We marked the pitch: four jackets for four goalposts,
That was all. The corners and the squares
Were there like longitude and latitude
Under the bumpy ground, to be
Agreed about or disagreed about
When the time came. And then we picked the teams
And crossed the line our called names drew between us.

Youngsters shouting their heads off in a field
As the light died and they kept on playing
Because by then they were playing in their heads
And the actual kicked ball came to them
Like a dream heaviness, and their own hard
Breathing in the dark and skids on grass
Sounded like effort in another world . . .
It was quick and constant, a game that never need
Be played out. Some limit had been passed,
There was fleetness, furtherance, untiredness
In time that was extra, unforeseen and free.

II

You also loved lines pegged out in the garden,
The spade nicking the first straight edge along
The tight white string. Or string stretched perfectly
To make the outline of a house foundation,
Pale timber battens set at right angles

[3]

For every corner, each freshly sawn new board
Spick and span in the oddly passive grass.
Or the imaginary line straight down
A field of grazing, to be ploughed open
From the rod stuck in one headrig to the rod
Stuck in the other.

III

All these things entered you
As if they were both the door and what came through it.
They marked the spot, marked time and held it open.
A mower parted the bronze sea of corn.
A windlass hauled the centre out of water.
Two men with a cross-cut kept it swimming
Into a felled beech backwards and forwards
So that they seemed to row the steady earth.

Man and Boy

'Catch the old one first,'
(My father's joke was also old, and heavy
And predictable). 'Then the young ones
Will all follow, and Bob's your uncle.'

On slow bright river evenings, the sweet time
Made him afraid we'd take too much for granted
And so our spirits must be lightly checked.

Blessed be down-to-earth! Blessed be highs!
Blessed be the detachment of dumb love
In that broad-backed, low-set man
Who feared debt all his life, but now and then
Could make a splash like the salmon he said was
'As big as a wee pork pig by the sound of it'.

In earshot of the pool where the salmon jumped
Back through its own unheard concentric soundwaves
A mower leans forever on his scythe.

He has mown himself to the centre of the field
And stands in a final perfect ring
Of sunlit stubble.

'Go and tell your father,' the mower says
(He said it to my father who told me),
'I have it mowed as clean as a new sixpence.'

My father is a barefoot boy with news,
Running at eye-level with weeds and stooks
On the afternoon of his own father's death.

The open, black half of the half-door waits.
I feel much heat and hurry in the air.
I feel his legs and quick heels far away

And strange as my own – when he will piggyback me
At a great height, light-headed and thin-boned,
Like a witless elder rescued from the fire.

Seeing Things

Inishbofin on a Sunday morning.
Sunlight, turfsmoke, seagulls, boatslip, diesel.
One by one we were being handed down
Into a boat that dipped and shilly-shallied
Scaresomely every time. We sat tight
On short cross-benches, in nervous twos and threes,
Obedient, newly close, nobody speaking
Except the boatmen, as the gunwales sank
And seemed they might ship water any minute.
The sea was very calm but even so,
When the engine kicked and our ferryman
Swayed for balance, reaching for the tiller,
I panicked at the shiftiness and heft
Of the craft itself. What guaranteed us –
That quick response and buoyancy and swim –
Kept me in agony. All the time
As we went sailing evenly across
The deep, still, seeable-down-into water,
It was as if I looked from another boat
Sailing through air, far up, and could see
How riskily we fared into the morning,
And loved in vain our bare, bowed, numbered heads.

Claritas. The dry-eyed Latin word
Is perfect for the carved stone of the water
Where Jesus stands up to his unwet knees
And John the Baptist pours out more water
Over his head: all this in bright sunlight
On the façade of a cathedral. Lines
Hard and thin and sinuous represent
The flowing river. Down between the lines
Little antic fish are all go. Nothing else.
And yet in that utter visibility
The stone's alive with what's invisible:
Waterweed, stirred sand-grains hurrying off,
The shadowy, unshadowed stream itself.
All afternoon, heat wavered on the steps
And the air we stood up to our eyes in wavered
Like the zig-zag hieroglyph for life itself.

III

Once upon a time my undrowned father
Walked into our yard. He had gone to spray
Potatoes in a field on the riverbank
And wouldn't bring me with him. The horse-sprayer
Was too big and new-fangled, bluestone might
Burn me in the eyes, the horse was fresh, I
Might scare the horse, and so on. I threw stones
At a bird on the shed roof, as much for
The clatter of the stones as anything,
But when he came back, I was inside the house
And saw him out the window, scatter-eyed
And daunted, strange without his hat,
His step unguided, his ghosthood immanent.
When he was turning on the riverbank,
The horse had rusted and reared up and pitched
Cart and sprayer and everything off balance
So the whole rig went over into a deep
Whirlpool, hoofs, chains, shafts, cartwheels, barrel
And tackle, all tumbling off the world,
And the hat already merrily swept along
The quieter reaches. That afternoon
I saw him face to face, he came to me
With his damp footprints out of the river,
And there was nothing between us there
That might not still be happily ever after.

An August Night

His hands were warm and small and knowledgeable.
When I saw them again last night, they were two ferrets,
Playing all by themselves in a moonlit field.

Field of Vision

I remember this woman who sat for years
In a wheelchair, looking straight ahead
Out the window at sycamore trees unleafing
And leafing at the far end of the lane.

Straight out past the TV in the corner,
The stunted, agitated hawthorn bush,
The same small calves with their backs to wind and rain,
The same acre of ragwort, the same mountain.

She was steadfast as the big window itself.
Her brow was clear as the chrome bits of the chair.
She never lamented once and she never
Carried a spare ounce of emotional weight.

Face to face with her was an education
Of the sort you got across a well-braced gate –
One of those lean, clean, iron, roadside ones
Between two whitewashed pillars, where you could see

Deeper into the country than you expected
And discovered that the field behind the hedge
Grew more distinctly strange as you kept standing
Focused and drawn in by what barred the way.

The Pitchfork

Of all implements, the pitchfork was the one
That came near to an imagined perfection:
When he tightened his raised hand and aimed with it,
It felt like a javelin, accurate and light.

So whether he played the warrior or the athlete
Or worked in earnest in the chaff and sweat,
He loved its grain of tapering, dark-flecked ash
Grown satiny from its own natural polish.

Riveted steel, turned timber, burnish, grain,
Smoothness, straightness, roundness, length and sheen.
Sweat-cured, sharpened, balanced, tested, fitted.
The springiness, the clip and dart of it.

And then when he thought of probes that reached the
    farthest,
He would see the shaft of a pitchfork sailing past
Evenly, imperturbably through space,
Its prongs starlit and absolutely soundless –

But has learned at last to follow that simple lead
Past its own aim, out to an other side
Where perfection – or nearness to it – is imagined
Not in the aiming but the opening hand.

The Settle Bed

Willed down, waited for, in place at last and for good.
Trunk-hasped, cart-heavy, painted an ignorant brown.
And pew-strait, bin-deep, standing four-square as an ark.

If I lie in it, I am cribbed in seasoned deal
Dry as the unkindled boards of a funeral ship.
My measure has been taken, my ear shuttered up.

Yet I hear an old sombre tide awash in the headboard:
Unpathetic *och ochs* and *och hohs,* the long bedtime
Sigh-life of Ulster, unwilling, unbeaten,

Protestant, Catholic, the Bible, the beads,
Late talks at gables by moonlight, boots on the hearth,
The small hours chimed sweetly away so next thing it was

The cock on the ridge-tiles.
                                    And now this is 'an inheritance' –
Upright, rudimentary, unshiftably planked
In the long long ago, yet willable forward

Again and again and again, cargoed with
Its own dumb, tongue-and-groove worthiness
And un-get-roundable weight. But to conquer that weight,

Imagine a dower of settle beds tumbled from heaven
Like some nonsensical vengeance come on the people,
Then learn from that harmless barrage that whatever is
   given

Can always be reimagined, however four-square,
Plank-thick, hull-stupid and out of its time
It happens to be. You are free as the lookout,

That far-seeing joker posted high over the fog,
Who declared by the time that he had got himself down
The actual ship had stolen away from beneath him.

from Glanmore Revisited

1 *Scrabble*

in memoriam Tom Delaney, archaeologist

Bare flags. Pump water. Winter-evening cold.
Our backs might never warm up but our faces
Burned from the hearth-blaze and the hot whiskeys.
It felt remembered even then, an old
Rightness half-imagined or foretold,
As green sticks hissed and spat into the ashes
And whatever rampaged out there couldn't reach us,
Firelit, shuttered, slated and stone-walled.

Year after year, our game of Scrabble: love
Taken for granted like any other word
That was chanced on and allowed within the rules.
So 'scrabble' let it be. Intransitive.
Meaning to scratch or rake at something hard.
Which is what he hears. Our scraping, clinking tools.

II *The Cot*

Scythe and axe and hedge-clippers, the shriek
Of the gate the children used to swing on,
Poker, scuttle, tongs, a gravel rake –
The old activity starts up again
But starts up differently. We're on our own
Years later in the same *locus amoenus*,
Tenants no longer, but in full possession
Of an emptied house and whatever keeps between us.

Which must be more than keepsakes, even though
The child's cot's back in place where Catherine
Woke in the dawn and answered *doodle doo*
To the rooster in the farm across the road –
And is the same cot I myself slept in
When the whole world was a farm that eked and crowed.

v *Lustral Sonnet*

Breaking and entering: from early on
Words that thrilled me far more than they scared me –
Even when I'd 'come into my own'
And owned a house, a man of property
Who lacked the proper outlook. I would never
Double-bar the door or lock the gate
Or draw the blinds or pull the curtains over
Or give 'security' a second thought.

But all changed when I took possession here
And had the old bed sawn on my instruction
Since the only way to move it down the stair
Was to cut the frame in two. A bad action,
So Greek with consequence, so dangerous,
Only pure words and deeds secure the house.

VII *The Skylight*

You were the one for skylights. I opposed
Cutting into the seasoned tongue-and-groove
Of pitch pine. I liked it low and closed,
Its claustrophobic, nest-up-in-the-roof
Effect. I liked the snuff-dry feeling,
The perfect, trunk-lid fit of the old ceiling.
Under there, it was all hutch and hatch.
The blue slates kept the heat like midnight thatch.

But when the slates came off, extravagant
Sky entered and held surprise wide open.
For days I felt like an inhabitant
Of that house where the man sick of the palsy
Was lowered through the roof, had his sins forgiven,
Was healed, took up his bed and walked away.

A Pillowed Head

Matutinal. Mother-of-pearl
Summer come early. Slashed carmines
And washed milky blues.

To be first on the road,
Up with the ground-mists and pheasants.
To be older and grateful

That this time you too were half-grateful
The pangs had begun – prepared
And clear-headed, foreknowing

The trauma, entering on it
With full consent of the will.
(The first time, dismayed and arrayed

In your cut-off white cotton gown,
You were more bride than earth-mother
Up on the stirrup-rigged bed,

Who were self-possessed now
To the point of a walk on the pier
Before you checked in.)

And then later on I half-fainted
When the little slapped palpable girl
Was handed to me; but as usual

Came to in two wide-open eyes
That had been dawned into farther
Than ever, and had outseen the last

Of all of those mornings of waiting
When your domed brow was one long held silence
And the dawn chorus anything but.

A Royal Prospect

On the day of their excursion up the Thames
To Hampton Court, they were nearly sunstruck.
She with her neck bared in a page-boy cut,
He all dreamy anyhow, wild for her
But pretending to be a thousand miles away,
Studying the boat's wake in the water.
And here are the photographs. Head to one side,
In her sleeveless blouse, one bare shoulder high
And one arm loose, a bird with a dropped wing
Surprised in cover. He looks at you straight,
Assailable, enamoured, full of vows,
Young dauphin in the once-upon-a-time.
And next the lowish red-brick Tudor frontage.
No more photographs, however, now
We are present there as the smell of grass
And suntan oil, standing like their sixth sense
Behind them at the entrance to the maze,
Heartbroken for no reason, willing them
To dare it to the centre they are lost for . . .
Instead, like reflections staggered through warped glass,
They reappear as in a black and white
Old grainy newsreel, where their pleasure-boat
Goes back spotlit across sunken bridges
And they alone are borne downstream unscathed,
Between mud banks where the wounded rave all night
At flameless blasts and echoless gunfire –
In all of which is ominously figured
Their free passage through historic times,
Like a silk train being brushed across a leper

Or the safe conduct of two royal favourites,
Unhindered and resented and bright-eyed.
So let them keep a tally of themselves
And be accountable when called upon
For although by every golden mean their lot
Is fair and due, pleas will be allowed
Against every right and title vested in them
(And in a court where mere innocuousness
Has never gained approval or acquittal).

Wheels within Wheels

I

The first real grip I ever got on things
Was when I learned the art of pedalling
(By hand) a bike turned upside down, and drove
Its back wheel preternaturally fast.
I loved the disappearance of the spokes,
The way the space between the hub and rim
Hummed with transparency. If you threw
A potato into it, the hooped air
Spun mush and drizzle back into your face;
If you touched it with a straw, the straw frittered.
Something about the way those pedal treads
Worked very palpably at first against you
And then began to sweep your hand ahead
Into a new momentum – that all entered me
Like an access of free power, as if belief
Caught up and spun the objects of belief
In an orbit coterminous with longing.

II

But enough was not enough. Who ever saw
The limit in the given anyhow?
In fields beyond our house there was a well
('The well' we called it. It was more a hole
With water in it, with small hawthorn trees
On one side, and a muddy, dungy ooze
On the other, all tramped through by cattle).

I loved that too. I loved the turbid smell,
The sump-life of the place like old chain oil.
And there, next thing, I brought my bicycle.
I stood its saddle and its handlebars
Into the soft bottom, I touched the tyres
To the water's surface, then turned the pedals
Until like a mill-wheel pouring at the treadles
(But here reversed and lashing a mare's tail)
The world-refreshing and immersed back wheel
Spun lace and dirt-suds there before my eyes
And showered me in my own regenerate clays.
For weeks I made a nimbus of old glit.
Then the hub jammed, rims rusted, the chain snapped.

III

Nothing rose to the occasion after that
Until, in a circus ring, drumrolled and spotlit,
Cowgirls wheeled in, each one immaculate
At the still centre of a lariat.
Perpetuum mobile. Sheer pirouette.
Tumblers. Jongleurs. Ring-a-rosies. *Stet!*

Fosterling

That heavy greenness fostered by water
JOHN MONTAGUE

At school I loved one picture's heavy greenness –
Horizons rigged with windmills' arms and sails.
The millhouses' still outlines. Their in-placeness
Still more in place when mirrored in canals.
I can't remember not ever having known
The immanent hydraulics of a land
Of *glar* and *glit* and floods at *dailigone*.
My silting hope. My lowlands of the mind.

Heaviness of being. And poetry
Sluggish in the doldrums of what happens.
Me waiting until I was nearly fifty
To credit marvels. Like the tree-clock of tin cans
The tinkers made. So long for air to brighten,
Time to be dazzled and the heart to lighten.

from Squarings

Lightenings

i

Shifting brilliancies. Then winter light
In a doorway, and on the stone doorstep
A beggar shivering in silhouette.

So the particular judgement might be set:
Bare wallstead and a cold hearth rained into –
Bright puddle where the soul-free cloud-life roams.

And after the commanded journey, what?
Nothing magnificent, nothing unknown.
A gazing out from far away, alone.

And it is not particular at all,
Just old truth dawning: there is no next-time-round.
Unroofed scope. Knowledge-freshening wind.

Roof it again. Batten down. Dig in.
Drink out of tin. Know the scullery cold,
A latch, a door-bar, forged tongs and a grate.

Touch the crossbeam, drive iron in a wall,
Hang a line to verify the plumb
From lintel, coping-stone and chimney-breast.

Relocate the bedrock in the threshold.
Take squarings from the recessed gable pane.
Make your study the unregarded floor.

Sink every impulse like a bolt. Secure
The bastion of sensation. Do not waver
Into language. Do not waver in it.

iii

Squarings? In the game of marbles, squarings
Were all those anglings, aimings, feints and squints
You were allowed before you'd shoot, all those

Hunkerings, tensings, pressures of the thumb,
Test-outs and pull-backs, re-envisagings,
All the ways your arms kept hoping towards

Blind certainties that were going to prevail
Beyond the one-off moment of the pitch.
A million million accuracies passed

Between your muscles' outreach and that space
Marked with three round holes and a drawn line.
You squinted out from a skylight of the world.

v

Three marble holes thumbed in the concrete road
Before the concrete hardened still remained
Three decades after the marble-player vanished

Into Australia. Three stops to play
The music of the arbitrary on.
Blow on them now and hear an undersong

Your levelled breath made once going over
The empty bottle. Improvise. Make free
Like old hay in its flimsy afterlife

High on a windblown hedge. Ocarina earth.
Three listening posts up on some hard-baked tier
Above the resonating amphorae.

Once, as a child, out in a field of sheep,
Thomas Hardy pretended to be dead
And lay down flat among their dainty shins.

In that sniffed-at, bleated-into, grassy space
He experimented with infinity.
His small cool brow was like an anvil waiting

For sky to make it sing the perfect pitch
Of his dumb being, and that stir he caused
In the fleece-hustle was the original

Of a ripple that would travel eighty years
Outward from there, to be the same ripple
Inside him at its last circumference.

vii

(I misremembered. He went down on all fours,
Florence Emily says, crossing a ewe-leaze.
Hardy sought the creatures face to face,

Their witless eyes and liability
To panic made him feel less alone,
Made proleptic sorrow stand a moment

Over him, perfectly known and sure.
And then the flock's dismay went swimming on
Into the blinks and murmurs and deflections

He'd know at parties in renowned old age
When sometimes he imagined himself a ghost
And circulated with that new perspective.)

The annals say: when the monks of Clonmacnoise
Were all at prayers inside the oratory
A ship appeared above them in the air.

The anchor dragged along behind so deep
It hooked itself into the altar rails
And then, as the big hull rocked to a standstill,

A crewman shinned and grappled down the rope
And struggled to release it. But in vain.
'This man can't bear our life here and will drown,'

The abbot said, 'unless we help him.' So
They did, the freed ship sailed, and the man climbed back
Out of the marvellous as he had known it.

A boat that did not rock or wobble once
Sat in long grass one Sunday afternoon
In nineteen forty-one or two. The heat

Out on Lough Neagh and in where cattle stood
Jostling and skittering near the hedge
Grew redolent of the tweed skirt and tweed sleeve

I nursed on. I remember little treble
Timber-notes their smart heels struck from planks,
Me cradled in an elbow like a secret

Open now as the eye of heaven was then
Above three sisters talking, talking steady
In a boat the ground still falls and falls from under.

x

Overhang of grass and seedling birch
On the quarry face. Rock-hob where you watched
All that cargoed brightness travelling

Above and beyond and sumptuously across
The water in its clear deep dangerous holes
On the quarry floor. Ultimate

Fathomableness, ultimate
Stony up-againstness: could you reconcile
What was diaphanous there with what was massive?

Were you equal to or were you opposite
To build-ups so promiscuous and weightless?
Shield your eyes, look up and face the music.

And lightening? One meaning of that
Beyond the usual sense of alleviation,
Illumination, and so on, is this:

A phenomenal instant when the spirit flares
With pure exhilaration before death –
The good thief in us harking to the promise!

So paint him on Christ's right hand, on a promontory
Scanning empty space, so body-racked he seems
Untranslatable into the bliss

Ached for at the moon-rim of his forehead,
By nail-craters on the dark side of his brain:
This day thou shalt be with Me in Paradise.

Settings

Hazel stealth. A trickle in the culvert.
Athletic sealight on the doorstep slab,
On the sea itself, on silent roofs and gables.

Whitewashed suntraps. Hedges hot as chimneys.
Chairs on all fours. A plate-rack braced and laden.
The fossil poetry of hob and slate.

Desire within its moat, dozing at ease –
Like a gorged cormorant on the rock at noon,
Exiled and in tune with the big glitter.

Re-enter this as the adult of solitude,
The silence-forder and the definite
Presence you sensed withdrawing first time round.

xiv

One afternoon I was seraph on gold leaf.
I stood on the railway sleepers hearing larks,
Grasshoppers, cuckoos, dog-barks, trainer planes

Cutting and modulating and drawing off.
Heat wavered on the immaculate line
And shine of the cogged rails. On either side,

Dog daisies stood like vestals, the hot stones
Were clover-meshed and streaked with engine oil.
Air spanned, passage waited, the balance rode,

Nothing prevailed, whatever was in store
Witnessed itself already taking place
In a time marked by assent and by hiatus.

And strike this scene in gold too, in relief,
So that a greedy eye cannot exhaust it:
Stable straw, Rembrandt-gleam and burnish

Where my father bends to a tea-chest packed with salt,
The hurricane lamp held up at eye-level
In his bunched left fist, his right hand foraging

For the unbleeding, vivid-fleshed bacon,
Home-cured hocks pulled up into the light
For pondering a while and putting back.

That night I owned the piled grain of Egypt.
I watched the sentry's torchlight on the hoard.
I stood in the door, unseen and blazed upon.

xix

Memory as a building or a city,
Well lighted, well laid out, appointed with
Tableaux vivants and costumed effigies –

Statues in purple cloaks, or painted red,
Ones wearing crowns, ones smeared with mud or blood:
So that the mind's eye could haunt itself

With fixed associations and learn to read
Its own contents in meaningful order,
Ancient textbooks recommended that

Familiar places be linked deliberately
With a code of images. You knew the portent
In each setting, you blinked and concentrated.

Where does spirit live? Inside or outside
Things remembered, made things, things unmade?
What came first, the seabird's cry or the soul

Imagined in the dawn cold when it cried?
Where does it roost at last? On dungy sticks
In a jackdaw's nest up in the old stone tower

Or a marble bust commanding the parterre?
How habitable is perfected form?
And how inhabited the windy light?

What's the use of a held note or held line
That cannot be assailed for reassurance?
(Set questions for the ghost of W. B.)

Deserted harbour stillness. Every stone
Clarified and dormant under water,
The harbour wall a masonry of silence.

Fullness. Shimmer. Laden high Atlantic
The moorings barely stirred in, very slight
Clucking of the swell against boat boards.

Perfected vision: cockle minarets
Consigned down there with green-slicked bottle glass,
Shell-debris and a reddened bud of sandstone.

Air and ocean known as antecedents
Of each other. In apposition with
Omnipresence, equilibrium, brim.

Crossings

xxvii

Everything flows. Even a solid man,
A pillar to himself and to his trade,
All yellow boots and stick and soft felt hat,

Can sprout wings at the ankle and grow fleet
As the god of fair days, stone posts, roads and crossroads,
Guardian of travellers and psychopomp.

'Look for a man with an ashplant on the boat,'
My father told his sister setting out
For London, 'and stay near him all night

And you'll be safe.' Flow on, flow on
The journey of the soul with its soul guide
And the mysteries of dealing-men with sticks!

Scissor-and-slap abruptness of a latch.
Its coldness to the thumb. Its see-saw lift
And drop and innocent harshness.

Which is a music of binding and of loosing
Unheard in this generation, but there to be
Called up or called down at a touch renewed.

Once the latch pronounces, roof
Is original again, threshold fatal,
The sanction powerful as the foreboding.

Your footstep is already known, so bow
Just a little, raise your right hand,
Make impulse one with wilfulness, and enter.

On St Brigid's Day the new life could be entered
By going through her girdle of straw rope:
The proper way for men was right leg first,

Then right arm and right shoulder, head, then left
Shoulder, arm and leg. Women drew it down
Over the body and stepped out of it.

The open they came into by these moves
Stood opener, hoops came off the world,
They could feel the February air

Still soft above their heads and imagine
The limp rope fray and flare like wind-borne gleanings
Or an unhindered goldfinch over ploughland.

xxxii

Running water never disappointed.
Crossing water always furthered something.
Stepping stones were stations of the soul.

A kesh could mean the track some called a *causey*
Raised above the wetness of the bog,
Or the causey where it bridged old drains and streams.

It steadies me to tell these things. Also
I cannot mention keshes or the ford
Without my father's shade appearing to me

On a path towards sunset, eyeing spades and clothes
That turf-cutters stowed perhaps or souls cast off
Before they crossed the log that spans the burn.

xxxiii

Be literal a moment. Recollect
Walking out on what had been emptied out
After he died, turning your back and leaving.

That morning tiles were harder, windows colder,
The raindrops on the pane more scourged, the grass
Barer to the sky, more wind-harrowed,

Or so it seemed. The house that he had planned
'Plain, big, straight, ordinary, you know',
A paradigm of rigour and correction,

Rebuke to fanciness and shrine to limit,
Stood firmer than ever for its own idea
Like a printed X-ray for the X-rayed body.

Yeats said, *To those who see spirits, human skin*
for a long time afterwards appears most coarse.
The face I see that all falls short of since

Passes down an aisle: I share the bus
From San Francisco Airport into Berkeley
With one other passenger, who's dropped

At the Treasure Island military base
Half-way across Bay Bridge. Vietnam-bound,
He could have been one of the newly dead come back,

Unsurprisable but still disappointed,
Having to bear his farm-boy self again,
His shaving cuts, his otherworldly brow.

And yes, my friend, we too walked through a valley.
Once. In darkness. With all the streetlamps off.
As danger gathered and the march dispersed.

Scene from Dante, made more memorable
By one of his head-clearing similes –
Fireflies, say, since the policemen's torches

Clustered and flicked and tempted us to trust
Their unpredictable, attractive light.
We were like herded shades who had to cross

And did cross, in a panic, to the car
Parked as we'd left it, that gave when we got in
Like Charon's boat under the faring poets.

Squarings

In famous poems by the sage Han Shan,
Cold Mountain is a place that can also mean
A state of mind. Or different states of mind

At different times, for the poems seem
One-off, impulsive, the kind of thing that starts
I have sat here facing the Cold Mountain

For twenty-nine years, or *There is no path*
That goes all the way – enviable stuff,
Unfussy and believable.

Talking about it isn't good enough
But quoting from it at least demonstrates
The virtue of an art that knows its mind.

xxxviii

We climbed the Capitol by moonlight, felt
The transports of temptation on the heights:
We were privileged and belated and we knew it.

Then something in me moved to prophesy
Against the beloved stand-offishness of marble
And all emulation of stone-cut verses.

'Down with form triumphant, long live,' (said I)
'Form mendicant and convalescent. We attend
The come-back of pure water and the prayer-wheel.'

To which a voice replied, 'Of course we do.
But the others are in the Forum Café waiting,
Wondering where we are. What'll you have?'

xxxix

When you sat, far-eyed and cold, in the basalt throne
Of 'the wishing chair' at Giant's Causeway,
The small of your back made very solid sense.

Like a papoose at sap-time strapped to a maple tree,
You gathered force out of the world-tree's hardness.
If you stretched your hand forth, things might turn to stone.

But you were only goose-fleshed skin and bone,
The rocks and wonder of the world were only
Lava crystallized, salts of the earth

The wishing chair gave a savour to, its kelp
And ozone freshening your outlook
Beyond the range you thought you'd settled for.

xl

I was four but I turned four hundred maybe
Encountering the ancient dampish feel
Of a clay floor. Maybe four thousand even.

Anyhow, there it was. Milk poured for cats
In a rank puddle-place, splash-darkened mould
Around the terracotta water-crock.

Ground of being. Body's deep obedience
To all its shifting tenses. A half-door
Opening directly into starlight.

Out of that earth house I inherited
A stack of singular, cold memory-weights
To load me, hand and foot, in the scale of things.

xli

Sand-bed, they said. And gravel-bed. Before
I knew river shallows or river pleasures
I knew the ore of longing in those words.

The places I go back to have not failed
But will not last. Waist-deep in cow-parsley,
I re-enter the swim, riding or quelling

The very currents memory is composed of,
Everything accumulated ever
As I took squarings from the tops of bridges

Or the banks of self at evening.
Lick of fear. Sweet transience. Flirt and splash.
Crumpled flow the sky-dipped willows trailed in.

xlii

Heather and kesh and turf stacks reappear
Summer by summer still, grasshoppers and all,
The same yet rarer: fields of the nearly blessed

Where gaunt ones in their shirtsleeves stooped and dug
Or stood alone at dusk surveying bog-banks –
Apparitions now, yet active still

And territorial, still sure of their ground,
Still interested, not knowing how far
The country of the shades has been pushed back,

How long the lark has stopped outside these fields
And only seems unstoppable to them
Caught like a far hill in a freak of sunshine.

xliii

Choose one set of tracks and track a hare
Until the prints stop, just like that, in snow.
End of the line. Smooth drifts. Where did she go?

Back on her tracks, of course, then took a spring
Yards off to the side; clean break; no scent or sign.
She landed in her form and ate the snow.

Consider too the ancient hieroglyph
Of 'hare and zig-zag', which meant 'to exist',
To be on the *qui vive*, weaving and dodging

Like our friend who sprang (goodbye) beyond our ken
And missed a round at last (but of course he'd stood it):
The shake-the-heart, the dew-hammer, the far-eyed.

xliv

All gone into the world of light? Perhaps
As we read the line sheer forms do crowd
The starry vestibule. Otherwise

They do not. What lucency survives
Is blanched as worms on nightlines I would lift,
Ungratified if always well prepared

For the nothing there – which was only what had been there.
Although in fact it is more like a caught line snapping,
That moment of admission of *All gone,*

When the rod butt loses touch and the tip drools
And eddies swirl a dead leaf past in silence
Swifter (it seems) than the water's passage.

xlv

For certain ones what was written may come true:
They shall live on in the distance
At the mouths of rivers.

For our ones, no. They will re-enter
Dryness that was heaven on earth to them,
Happy to eat the scones baked out of clay.

For some, perhaps, the delta's reed-beds
And cold bright-footed seabirds always wheeling.
For our ones, snuff

And hob-soot and the heat off ashes.
And a judge who comes between them and the sun
In a pillar of radiant house-dust.

xlvi

Mountain air from the mountain up behind;
Out front, the end-of-summer, stone-walled fields;
And in a slated house the fiddle going

Like a flat stone skimmed at sunset
Or the irrevocable slipstream of flat earth
Still fleeing behind space.

Was music once a proof of God's existence?
As long as it admits things beyond measure,
That supposition stands.

So let the ear attend like a farmhouse window
In placid light, where the extravagant
Passed once under full sail into the longed-for.

xlvii

The visible sea at a distance from the shore
Or beyond the anchoring grounds
Was called the offing.

The emptier it stood, the more compelled
The eye that scanned it.
But once you turned your back on it, your back

Was suddenly all eyes like Argus's.
Then, when you'd look again, the offing felt
Untrespassed still, and yet somehow vacated

As if a lambent troop that exercised
On the borders of your vision had withdrawn
Behind the skyline to manoeuvre and regroup.

xlviii

Strange how things in the offing, once they're sensed,
Convert to things foreknown;
And how what's come upon is manifest

Only in light of what has been gone through.
Seventh heaven may be
The whole truth of a sixth sense come to pass.

At any rate, when light breaks over me
The way it did on the road beyond Coleraine
Where wind got saltier, the sky more hurried

And silver lamé shivered on the Bann
Out in mid-channel between the painted poles,
That day I'll be in step with what escaped me.

The Rain Stick

for Beth and Rand

Up-end the rain stick and what happens next
Is a music that you never would have known
To listen for. In a cactus stalk

Downpour, sluice-rush, spillage and backwash
Come flowing through. You stand there like a pipe
Being played by water, you shake it again lightly

And diminuendo runs through all its scales
Like a gutter stopping trickling. And now here comes
A sprinkle of drops out of the freshened leaves,

Then subtle little wets off grass and daisies;
Then glitter-drizzle, almost-breaths of air.
Up-end the stick again. What happens next

Is undiminished for having happened once,
Twice, ten, a thousand times before.
Who cares if all the music that transpires

Is the fall of grit or dry seeds through a cactus?
You are like a rich man entering heaven
Through the ear of a raindrop. Listen now again.

Mint

It looked like a clump of small dusty nettles
Growing wild at the gable of the house
Beyond where we dumped our refuse and old bottles:
Unverdant ever, almost beneath notice.

But, to be fair, it also spelled promise
And newness in the back yard of our life
As if something callow yet tenacious
Sauntered in green alleys and grew rife.

The snip of scissor blades, the light of Sunday
Mornings when the mint was cut and loved:
My last things will be first things slipping from me.
Yet let all things go free that have survived.

Let the smells of mint go heady and defenceless
Like inmates liberated in that yard.
Like the disregarded ones we turned against
Because we'd failed them by our disregard.

A Sofa in the Forties

All of us on the sofa in a line, kneeling
Behind each other, eldest down to youngest,
Elbows going like pistons, for this was a train

And between the jamb-wall and the bedroom door
Our speed and distance were inestimable.
First we shunted, then we whistled, then

Somebody collected the invisible
For tickets and very gravely punched it
As carriage after carriage under us

Moved faster, *chooka-chook,* the sofa legs
Went giddy and the unreachable ones
Far out on the kitchen floor began to wave.

*

Ghost-train? Death-gondola? The carved, curved ends,
Black leatherette and ornate gauntness of it
Made it seem the sofa had achieved

Flotation. Its castors on tiptoe,
Its braid and fluent backboard gave it airs
Of superannuated pageantry:

When visitors endured it, straight-backed,
When it stood off in its own remoteness,
When the insufficient toys appeared on it

On Christmas mornings, it held out as itself,
Potentially heavenbound, earthbound for sure,
Among things that might add up or let you down.

*

We entered history and ignorance
Under the wireless shelf. *Yippee-i-ay,*
Sang 'The Riders of the Range', HERE IS THE NEWS,

Said the absolute speaker. Between him and us
A great gulf was fixed where pronunciation
Reigned tyrannically. The aerial wire

Swept from a treetop down in through a hole
Bored in the windowframe. When it moved in wind,
The sway of language and its furtherings

Swept and swayed in us like nets in water
Or the abstract, lonely curve of distant trains
As we entered history and ignorance.

*

We occupied our seats with all our might,
Fit for the uncomfortableness.
Constancy was its own reward already.

Out in front, on the big upholstered arm,
Somebody craned to the side, driver or
Fireman, wiping his dry brow with the air

Of one who had run the gauntlet. We were
The last thing on his mind, it seemed; we sensed
A tunnel coming up where we'd pour through

Like unlit carriages through fields at night,
Our only job to sit, eyes straight ahead,
And be transported and make engine noise.

Keeping Going

for Hugh

The piper coming from far away is you
With a whitewash brush for a sporran
Wobbling round you, a kitchen chair
Upside down on your shoulder, your right arm
Pretending to tuck the bag beneath your elbow,
Your pop-eyes and big cheeks nearly bursting
With laughter, but keeping the drone going on
Interminably, between catches of breath.

*

The whitewash brush. An old blanched skirted thing
On the back of the byre door, biding its time
Until spring airs spelled lime in a work-bucket
And a potstick to mix it in with water.
Those smells brought tears to the eyes, we inhaled
A kind of greeny burning and thought of brimstone.
But the slop of the actual job
Of brushing walls, the watery grey
Being lashed on in broad swatches, then drying out
Whiter and whiter, all that worked like magic.
Where had we come from, what was this kingdom
We knew we'd been restored to? Our shadows
Moved on the wall and a tar border glittered
The full length of the house, a black divide
Like a freshly opened, pungent, reeking trench.

*

Piss at the gable, the dead will congregate.
But separately. The women after dark,

Hunkering there a moment before bedtime,
The only time the soul was let alone,
The only time that face and body calmed
In the eye of heaven.
                              Buttermilk and urine,
The pantry, the housed beasts, the listening bedroom.
We were all together there in a foretime,
In a knowledge that might not translate beyond
Those wind-heaved midnights we still cannot be sure
Happened or not. It smelled of hill-fort clay
And cattle dung. When the thorn tree was cut down
You broke your arm. I shared the dread
When a strange bird perched for days on the byre roof.

                              *

That scene, with Macbeth helpless and desperate
In his nightmare – when he meets the hags again
And sees the apparitions in the pot –
I felt at home with that one all right. Hearth,
Steam and ululation, the smoky hair
Curtaining a cheek. 'Don't go near bad boys
In that college that you're bound for. Do you hear me?
Do you hear me speaking to you? Don't forget!'
And then the potstick quickening the gruel,
The steam crown swirled, everything intimate
And fear-swathed brightening for a moment,
Then going dull and fatal and away.

                              *

Grey matter like gruel flecked with blood
In spatters on the whitewash. A clean spot
Where his head had been, other stains subsumed
In the parched wall he leant his back against

That morning like any other morning,
Part-time reservist, toting his lunch-box.
A car came slow down Castle Street, made the halt,
Crossed the Diamond, slowed again and stopped
Level with him, although it was not his lift.
And then he saw an ordinary face
For what it was and a gun in his own face.
His right leg was hooked back, his sole and heel
Against the wall, his right knee propped up steady,
So he never moved, just pushed with all his might
Against himself, then fell past the tarred strip,
Feeding the gutter with his copious blood.

*

My dear brother, you have good stamina.
You stay on where it happens. Your big tractor
Pulls up at the Diamond, you wave at people,
You shout and laugh above the revs, you keep
Old roads open by driving on the new ones.
You called the piper's sporrans whitewash brushes
And then dressed up and marched us through the kitchen,
But you cannot make the dead walk or right wrong.
I see you at the end of your tether sometimes,
In the milking parlour, holding yourself up
Between two cows until your turn goes past,
Then coming to in the smell of dung again
And wondering, is this all? As it was
In the beginning, is now and shall be?
Then rubbing your eyes and seeing our old brush
Up on the byre door, and keeping going.

Two Lorries

It's raining on black coal and warm wet ashes.
There are tyre-marks in the yard, Agnew's old lorry
Has all its cribs down and Agnew the coalman
With his Belfast accent's sweet-talking my mother.
Would she ever go to a film in Magherafelt?
But it's raining and he still has half the load

To deliver farther on. This time the lode
Our coal came from was silk-black, so the ashes
Will be the silkiest white. The Magherafelt
(Via Toomebridge) bus goes by. The half-stripped lorry
With its emptied, folded coal-bags moves my mother:
The tasty ways of a leather-aproned coalman!

And films no less! The conceit of a coalman . . .
She goes back in and gets out the black lead
And emery paper, this nineteen-forties mother,
All business round her stove, half-wiping ashes
With a backhand from her cheek as the bolted lorry
Gets revved and turned and heads for Magherafelt

And the last delivery. Oh, Magherafelt!
Oh, dream of red plush and a city coalman
As time fastforwards and a different lorry
Groans into shot, up Broad Street, with a payload
That will blow the bus station to dust and ashes . . .
After that happened, I'd a vision of my mother,

A revenant on the bench where I would meet her
In that cold-floored waiting-room in Magherafelt,
Her shopping bags full up with shovelled ashes.
Death walked out past her like a dust-faced coalman
Refolding body-bags, plying his load
Empty upon empty, in a flurry

Of motes and engine-revs, but which lorry
Was it now? Young Agnew's or that other,
Heavier, deadlier one, set to explode
In a time beyond her time in Magherafelt . . .
So tally bags and sweet-talk darkness, coalman.
Listen to the rain spit in new ashes

As you heft a load of dust that was Magherafelt,
Then reappear from your lorry as my mother's
Dreamboat coalman filmed in silk-white ashes.

Damson

Gules and cement dust. A matte tacky blood
On the bricklayer's knuckles, like the damson stain
That seeped through his packed lunch.

                                        A full hod stood
Against the mortared wall, his big bright trowel
In his left hand (for once) was pointing down
As he marvelled at his right, held high and raw:
King of the castle, scaffold-stepper, shown
Bleeding to the world.

                        Wound that I saw
In glutinous colour fifty years ago –
Damson as omen, weird, a dream to read –
Is weeping with the held-at-arm's-length dead
From everywhere and nowhere, here and now.

                        *

Over and over, the slur, the scrape and mix
As he trowelled and retrowelled and laid down
Courses of glum mortar. Then the bricks
Jiggled and settled, tocked and tapped in line.
I loved especially the trowel's shine,
Its edge and apex always coming clean
And brightening itself by mucking in.
It looked light but felt heavy as a weapon,
Yet when he lifted it there was no strain.
It was all point and skim and float and glisten
Until he washed and lapped it tight in sacking
Like a cult blade that had to be kept hidden.

                        *

Ghosts with their tongues out for a lick of blood
Are crowding up the ladder, all unhealed,
And some of them still rigged in bloody gear.
Drive them back to the doorstep or the road
Where they lay in their own blood once, in the hot
Nausea and last gasp of dear life.
Trowel-wielder, woundie, drive them off
Like Odysseus in Hades lashing out
With his sword that dug the trench and cut the throat
Of the sacrificial lamb.
                              But not like him –
Builder, not sacker, your shield the mortar board –
Drive them back to the wine-dark taste of home,
The smell of damsons simmering in a pot,
Jam ladled thick and steaming down the sunlight.

Weighing In

The 56 lb weight. A solid iron
Unit of negation. Stamped and cast
With an inset, rung-thick, moulded, short crossbar

For a handle. Squared-off and harmless-looking
Until you tried to lift it, then a socket-ripping,
Life-belittling force –

Gravity's black box, the immovable
Stamp and squat and square-root of dead weight.
Yet balance it

Against another one placed on a weighbridge –
On a well-adjusted, freshly greased weighbridge –
And everything trembled, flowed with give and take.

*

And this is all the good tidings amount to:
This principle of bearing, bearing up
And bearing out, just having to

Balance the intolerable in others
Against our own, having to abide
Whatever we settled for and settled into

Against our better judgement. Passive
Suffering makes the world go round.
Peace on earth, men of good will, all that

Holds good only as long as the balance holds,
The scales ride steady and the angels' strain
Prolongs itself at an unearthly pitch.

*

To refuse the other cheek. To cast the stone.
Not to do so some time, not to break with
The obedient one you hurt yourself into

Is to fail the hurt, the self, the ingrown rule.
Prophesy who struck thee! When soldiers mocked
Blindfolded Jesus and he didn't strike back

They were neither shamed nor edified, although
Something was made manifest – the power
Of power not exercised, of hope inferred

By the powerless forever. Still, for Jesus' sake,
Do me a favour, would you, just this once?
Prophesy, give scandal, cast the stone.

*

Two sides to every question, yes, yes, yes . . .
But every now and then, just weighing in
Is what it must come down to, and without

Any self-exculpation or self-pity.
Alas, one night when follow-through was called for
And a quick hit would have fairly rankled,

You countered that it was my narrowness
That kept me keen, so got a first submission.
I held back when I should have drawn blood

And that way (*mea culpa*) lost an edge.
A deep mistaken chivalry, old friend.
At this stage only foul play cleans the slate.

St Kevin and the Blackbird

And then there was St Kevin and the blackbird.
The saint is kneeling, arms stretched out, inside
His cell, but the cell is narrow, so

One turned-up palm is out the window, stiff
As a crossbeam, when a blackbird lands
And lays in it and settles down to nest.

Kevin feels the warm eggs, the small breast, the tucked
Neat head and claws and, finding himself linked
Into the network of eternal life,

Is moved to pity: now he must hold his hand
Like a branch out in the sun and rain for weeks
Until the young are hatched and fledged and flown.

*

And since the whole thing's imagined anyhow,
Imagine being Kevin. Which is he?
Self-forgetful or in agony all the time

From the neck on out down through his hurting forearms?
Are his fingers sleeping? Does he still feel his knees?
Or has the shut-eyed blank of underearth

Crept up through him? Is there distance in his head?
Alone and mirrored clear in love's deep river,
'To labour and not to seek reward,' he prays,

A prayer his body makes entirely
For he has forgotten self, forgotten bird
And on the riverbank forgotten the river's name.

from The Flight Path

4

The following for the record, in the light
Of everything before and since:
One bright May morning, nineteen seventy-nine,
Just off the red-eye special from New York,
I'm on the train for Belfast. Plain, simple
Exhilaration at being back: the sea
At Skerries, the nuptial hawthorn bloom,
The trip north taking sweet hold like a chain
On every bodily sprocket.
                       Enter then –
As if he were some *film noir* border guard –
Enter this one I'd last met in a dream,
More grimfaced now than in the dream itself
When he'd flagged me down at the side of a
    mountain road,
Come up and leant his elbow on the roof
And explained through the open window of the car
That all I'd have to do was drive a van
Carefully in to the next customs post
At Pettigo, switch off, get out as if
I were on my way with dockets to the office –
But then instead I'd walk ten yards more down
Towards the main street and get in with – here
Another schoolfriend's name, a wink and smile,
I'd know him all right, he'd be in a Ford
And I'd be home in three hours' time, as safe
As houses . . .

So he enters and sits down
Opposite and goes for me head on.
'When, for fuck's sake, are you going to write
Something for us?' 'If I do write something,
Whatever it is, I'll be writing for myself.'
And that was that. Or words to that effect.

The jail walls all those months were smeared with shite.
Out of Long Kesh after his dirty protest
The red eyes were the eyes of Ciaran Nugent
Like something out of Dante's scurfy hell,
Drilling their way through the rhymes and images
Where I too walked behind the righteous Virgil,
As safe as houses and translating freely:
When he had said all this, his eyes rolled
And his teeth, like a dog's teeth clamping round a bone,
Bit into the skull and again took hold.

5

When I answered that I came from 'far away',
The policeman at the roadblock snapped, 'Where's that?'
He'd only half-heard what I said and thought
It was the name of some place up the country.

And now it is – both where I have been living
And where I left – a distance still to go
Like starlight that is light years on the go
From far away and takes light years arriving.

Mycenae Lookout

for Cynthia and Dimitri Hadzi

The ox is on my tongue
AESCHYLUS, *Agamemnon*

1 *The Watchman's War*

Some people wept, and not for sorrow – joy
That the king had armed and upped and sailed for Troy,
But inside me like struck sound in a gong
That killing-fest, the life-warp and world-wrong
It brought to pass, still augured and endured.
I'd dream of blood in bright webs in a ford,
Of bodies raining down like tattered meat
On top of me asleep – and me the lookout
The queen's command had posted and forgotten,
The blind spot her farsightedness relied on.
And then the ox would lurch against the gong
And deaden it and I would feel my tongue
Like the dropped gangplank of a cattle truck,
Trampled and rattled, running piss and muck,
All swimmy-trembly as the lick of fire,
A victory beacon in an abattoir . . .
Next thing then I would waken at a loss,
For all the world a sheepdog stretched in grass,
Exposed to what I knew, still honour-bound
To concentrate attention out beyond
The city and the border, on that line
Where the blaze would leap the hills when Troy had fallen.

My sentry work was fate, a home to go to,
An in-between-times that I had to row through
Year after year: when the mist would start
To lift off fields and inlets, when morning light
Would open like the grain of light being split,
Day in, day out, I'd come alive again,
Silent and sunned as an esker on a plain,
Up on my elbows, gazing, biding time
In my outpost on the roof . . . What was to come
Out of that ten years' wait that was the war
Flawed the black mirror of my frozen stare.
If a god of justice had reached down from heaven
For a strong beam to hang his scale-pans on
He would have found me tensed and ready-made.
I balanced between destiny and dread
And saw it coming, clouds bloodshot with the red
Of victory fires, the raw wound of that dawn
Igniting and erupting, bearing down
Like lava on a fleeing population . . .
Up on my elbows, head back, shutting out
The agony of Clytemnestra's love-shout
That rose through the palace like the yell of troops
Hurled by King Agamemnon from the ships.

2 *Cassandra*

No such thing
as innocent
bystanding.

Her soiled vest,
her little breasts,
her clipped, devast-

ated, scabbed
punk head,
the char-eyed

famine gawk –
she looked
camp-fucked

and simple.
People
could feel

a missed
trueness in them
focus,

a homecoming
in her dropped-wing,
half-calculating

bewilderment.
No such thing
as innocent.

Old King Cock-
of-the-Walk
was back,

King Kill-
the-Child-
and-Take-

What-Comes,
King Agamem-
non's drum-

balled, old buck's
stride was back.
And then her Greek

words came,
a lamb
at lambing time,

bleat of clair-
voyant dread,
the gene-hammer

and tread
of the roused god.
And the result-

ant shock desire
in bystanders
to do it to her

there and then.
Little rent
cunt of their guilt:

in she went
to the knife,
to the killer wife,

to the net over
her and her slaver,
the Troy reaver,

saying, 'A wipe
of the sponge,
that's it.

The shadow-hinge
swings unpredict-
ably and the light's

blanked out.'

3 *His Dawn Vision*

Cities of grass. Fort walls. The dumbstruck palace.
I'd come to with the night wind on my face,
Agog, alert again, but far, far less

Focused on victory than I should have been –
Still isolated in my old disdain
Of claques who always needed to be seen

And heard as the true Argives. Mouth athletes,
Quoting the oracle and quoting dates,
Petitioning, accusing, taking votes.

No element that should have carried weight
Out of the grievous distance would translate.
Our war stalled in the pre-articulate.

The little violets' heads bowed on their stems,
The pre-dawn gossamers, all dew and scrim
And star-lace, it was more through them

I felt the beating of the huge time-wound
We lived inside. My soul wept in my hand
When I would touch them, my whole being rained

Down on myself, I saw cities of grass,
Valleys of longing, tombs, a windswept brightness,
And far off, in a hilly, ominous place,

Small crowds of people watching as a man
Jumped a fresh earth-wall and another ran
Amorously, it seemed, to strike him down.

4 *The Nights*

They both needed to talk,
pretending what they needed
was my advice. Behind backs
each one of them confided
it was sexual overload
every time they did it –
and indeed from the beginning
(a child could have hardly missed it)
their real life was the bed.

The king should have been told,
but who was there to tell him
if not myself? I willed them
to cease and break the hold
of my cross-purposed silence
but still kept on, all smiles
to Aegisthus every morning,
much favoured and self-loathing.
The roof was like an eardrum.

The ox's tons of dumb
inertia stood, head-down
and motionless as a herm.
Atlas, watchmen's patron,
would come into my mind,
the only other one
up at all hours, ox-bowed
under his yoke of cloud
out there at the world's end.

The loft-floor where the gods
and goddesses took lovers
and made out endlessly
successfully, those thuds
and moans through the cloud cover
were wholly on his shoulders.
Sometimes I thought of us
apotheosized to boulders
called Aphrodite's Pillars.

High and low in those days
hit their stride together.
When the captains in the horse
felt Helen's hand caress
its wooden boards and belly
they nearly rode each other.
But in the end Troy's mothers
bore their brunt in alley,
bloodied cot and bed.
The war put all men mad,
horned, horsed or roof-posted,
the boasting and the bested.

My own mind was a bull-pen
where horned King Agamemnon
had stamped his weight in gold.
But when hills broke into flame
and the queen wailed on and came,
it was the king I sold.
I moved beyond bad faith:
for his bullion bars, his bonus
was a rope-net and a bloodbath.
And the peace had come upon us.

5 *His Reverie of Water*

At Troy, at Athens, what I most clearly
see and nearly smell
is the fresh water.

A filled bath, still unentered
and unstained, waiting behind housewalls
that the far cries of the butchered on the plain

keep dying into, until the hero comes
surging in incomprehensibly
to be attended to and be alone,

stripped to the skin, blood-plastered, moaning
and rocking, splashing, dozing off,
accommodated as if he were a stranger.

And the well at Athens too.
Or rather that old lifeline leading up
and down from the Acropolis

to the well itself, a set of timber steps
slatted in between the sheer cliff face
and a free-standing, covering spur of rock,

secret staircase the defenders knew
and the invaders found, where what was to be
Greek met Greek,

the ladder of the future
and the past, besieger and besieged,
the treadmill of assault

turned waterwheel, the rungs of stealth
and habit all the one
bare foot extended, searching.

And then this ladder of our own that ran
deep into a well-shaft being sunk
in broad daylight, men puddling at the source

through tawny mud, then coming back up
deeper in themselves for having been there,
like discharged soldiers testing the safe ground,

finders, keepers, seers of fresh water
in the bountiful round mouths of iron pumps
and gushing taps.

The Gravel Walks

River gravel. In the beginning, that.
High summer, and the angler's motorbike
Deep in roadside flowers, like a fallen knight
Whose ghost we'd lately questioned: 'Any luck?'

As the engines of the world prepared, green nuts
Dangled and clustered closer to the whirlpool.
The trees dipped down. The flints and sandstone-bits
Worked themselves smooth and smaller in a sparkle

Of shallow, hurrying barley-sugar water
Where minnows schooled that we scared when we
    played –
An eternity that ended once a tractor
Dropped its link-box in the gravel bed

And cement mixers began to come to life
And men in dungarees, like captive shades,
Mixed concrete, loaded, wheeled, turned, wheeled, as if
The Pharaoh's brickyards burned inside their heads.

*

Hoard and praise the verity of gravel.
Gems for the undeluded. Milt of earth.
Its plain, champing song against the shovel
Soundtests and sandblasts words like 'honest worth'.

Beautiful in or out of the river,
The kingdom of gravel was inside you too –
Deep down, far back, clear water running over
Pebbles of caramel, hailstone, mackerel-blue.

But the actual washed stuff kept you slow and steady
As you went stooping with your barrow full
Into an absolution of the body,
The shriven life tired bones and marrow feel.

So walk on air against your better judgement
Establishing yourself somewhere in between
Those solid batches mixed with grey cement
And a tune called 'The Gravel Walks' that conjures green.

Whitby-sur-Moyola

Caedmon too I was lucky to have known,
Back *in situ* there with his full bucket
And armfuls of clean straw, the perfect yardman,
Unabsorbed in what he had to do
But doing it perfectly, and watching you.
He had worked his angel stint. He was hard as nails
And all that time he'd been poeting with the harp
His real gift was the big ignorant roar
He could still let out of him, just bogging in
As if the sacred subjects were a herd
That had broken out and needed rounding up.
I never saw him once with his hands joined
Unless it was a case of eyes to heaven
And the quick sniff and test of fingertips
After he'd passed them through a sick beast's water.
Oh, Caedmon was the real thing all right.

'Poet's Chair'

for Carolyn Mulholland

Leonardo said: the sun has never
Seen a shadow. Now watch the sculptor move
Full circle round her next work, like a lover
In the sphere of shifting angles and fixed love.

I

Angling shadows of itself are what
Your 'Poet's Chair' stands to and rises out of
In its sun-stalked inner-city courtyard.
On the *qui vive* all the time, its four legs land
On their feet – cat's-foot, goat-foot, big soft splay-foot too;
Its straight back sprouts two bronze and leafy saplings.
Every flibbertigibbet in the town,
Old birds and boozers, late-night pissers, kissers,
All have a go at sitting on it some time.
It's the way the air behind them's winged and full,
The way a graft has seized their shoulder-blades
That makes them happy. Once out of nature,
They're going to come back in leaf and bloom
And angel step. Or something like that. *Leaves*
On a bloody chair! Would you believe it?

2

Next thing I see the chair in a white prison
With Socrates sitting on it, bald as a coot,
Discoursing in bright sunlight with his friends.
His time is short. The day his trial began

A verdant boat sailed for Apollo's shrine
In Delos, for the annual rite
Of commemoration. Until its wreathed
And creepered rigging re-enters Athens
Harbour, the city's life is holy.
No executions. No hemlock bowl. No tears
And none now as the poison does its work
And the expert jailer talks the company through
The stages of the numbness. Socrates
At the centre of the city and the day
Has proved the soul immortal. The bronze leaves
Cannot believe their ears, it is so silent.
Soon Crito will have to close his eyes and mouth,
But for the moment everything's an ache
Deferred, foreknown, imagined and most real.

3

My father's ploughing one, two, three, four sides
Of the lea ground where I sit all-seeing
At centre field, my back to the thorn tree
They never cut. The horses are all hoof
And burnished flank, I am all foreknowledge.
Of the poem as a ploughshare that turns time
Up and over. Of the chair in leaf
The fairy thorn is entering for the future.
Of being here for good in every sense.

The Swing

Fingertips just tipping you would send you
Every bit as far – once you got going –
As a big push in the back.
                              Sooner or later,
We all learned one by one to go sky high,
Backward and forward in the open shed,
Toeing and rowing and jack-knifing through air.

*

Not Fragonard. Nor Brueghel. It was more
Hans Memling's light of heaven off green grass,
Light over fields and hedges, the shed-mouth
Sunstruck and expectant, the bedding-straw
Piled to one side, like a Nativity
Foreground and background waiting for the figures.
And then, in the middle ground, the swing itself
With an old lopsided sack in the loop of it,
Perfectly still, hanging like pulley-slack,
A lure let down to tempt the soul to rise.

*

Even so, we favoured the earthbound. She
Sat there as majestic as an empress
Steeping her swollen feet one at a time
In the enamel basin, feeding it
Every now and again with an opulent
Steaming arc from a kettle on the floor
Beside her. The plout of that was music
To our ears, her smile a mitigation.

Whatever light the goddess had once shone
Around her favourite coming from the bath
Was what was needed then: there should have been
Fresh linen, ministrations by attendants,
Procession and amazement. Instead, she took
Each rolled elastic stocking and drew it on
Like the life she would not fail and was not
Meant for. And once, when she'd scoured the basin,
She came and sat to please us on the swing,
Neither out of place nor in her element,
Just tempted by it for a moment only,
Half-retrieving something half-confounded.
Instinctively we knew to let her be.

*

To start up by yourself, you hitched the rope
Against your backside and backed on into it
Until it tautened, then tiptoed and drove off
As hard as possible. You hurled a gathered thing
From the small of your own back into the air.
Your head swept low, you heard the whole shed creak.

*

We all learned one by one to go sky high.
Then townlands vanished into aerodromes,
Hiroshima made light of human bones,
Concorde's neb migrated towards the future.
So who were we to want to hang back there
In spite of all?
                    In spite of all, we sailed
Beyond ourselves and over and above
The rafters aching in our shoulderblades,
The give and take of branches in our arms.

Two Stick Drawings

1

Claire O'Reilly used her granny's stick –
A crook-necked one – to snare the highest briars
That always grew the ripest blackberries.
When it came to gathering, Persephone
Was in the halfpenny place compared to Claire.
She'd trespass and climb gates and walk the railway
Where sootflakes blew into convolvulus
And the train tore past with the stoker yelling
Like a balked king from his iron chariot.

2

With its drover's canes and blackthorns and ashplants,
The ledge of the back seat of my father's car
Had turned into a kind of stick-shop window,
But the only one who ever window-shopped
Was Jim of the hanging jaw, for Jim was simple
And rain or shine he'd make his desperate rounds
From windscreen to back window, hands held up
To both sides of his face, peering and groaning.
So every now and then the sticks would be
Brought out for him and stood up one by one
Against the front mudguard; and one by one
Jim would take the measure of them, sight
And wield and slice and poke and parry
The unhindering air; until he found
The true extension of himself in one

That made him jubilant. He'd run and crow,
Stooped forward, with his right elbow stuck out
And the stick held horizontal to the ground,
Angled across in front of him, as if
He were leashed to it and it drew him on
Like a harness rod of the inexorable.

A Call

'Hold on,' she said, 'I'll just run out and get him.
The weather here's so good, he took the chance
To do a bit of weeding.'
                              So I saw him
Down on his hands and knees beside the leek rig,
Touching, inspecting, separating one
Stalk from the other, gently pulling up
Everything not tapered, frail and leafless,
Pleased to feel each little weed-root break,
But rueful also . . .
                          Then found myself listening to
The amplified grave ticking of hall clocks
Where the phone lay unattended in a calm
Of mirror glass and sunstruck pendulums . . .

And found myself then thinking: if it were nowadays,
This is how Death would summon Everyman.

Next thing he spoke and I nearly said I loved him.

The Errand

'On you go now! Run, son, like the devil
And tell your mother to try
To find me a bubble for the spirit level
And a new knot for this tie.'

But still he was glad, I know, when I stood my ground,
Putting it up to him
With a smile that trumped his smile and his fool's errand,
Waiting for the next move in the game.

A Dog Was Crying Tonight in Wicklow Also

in memory of Donatus Nwoga

When human beings found out about death
They sent the dog to Chukwu with a message:
They wanted to be let back to the house of life.
They didn't want to end up lost forever
Like burnt wood disappearing into smoke
Or ashes that get blown away to nothing.
Instead, they saw their souls in a flock at twilight
Cawing and headed back for the same old roosts
And the same bright airs and wing-stretchings each
    morning.
Death would be like a night spent in the wood:
At first light they'd be back in the house of life.
(The dog was meant to tell all this to Chukwu).

But death and human beings took second place
When he trotted off the path and started barking
At another dog in broad daylight just barking
Back at him from the far bank of a river.

And that is how the toad reached Chukwu first,
The toad who'd overheard in the beginning
What the dog was meant to tell. 'Human beings,'
    he said
(And here the toad was trusted absolutely),
'Human beings want death to last forever.'

Then Chukwu saw the people's souls in birds
Coming towards him like black spots off the sunset

To a place where there would be neither roosts nor trees
Nor any way back to the house of life.
And his mind reddened and darkened all at once
And nothing that the dog would tell him later
Could change that vision. Great chiefs and great loves
In obliterated light, the toad in mud,
The dog crying out all night behind the corpse house.

The Strand

The dotted line my father's ashplant made
On Sandymount Strand
Is something else the tide won't wash away.

The Walk

Glamoured the road, the day, and him and her
And everywhere they took me. When we stepped out
Cobbles were riverbed, the Sunday air
A high stream-roof that moved in silence over
Rhododendrons in full bloom, foxgloves
And hemlock, robin-run-the-hedge, the hedge
With its deckled ivy and thick shadows –
Until the riverbed itself appeared,
Gravelly, shallowy, summery with pools,
And made a world rim that was not for crossing.
Love brought me that far by the hand, without
The slightest doubt or irony, dry-eyed
And knowledgeable, contrary as be damned;
Then just kept standing there, not letting go.

*

So here is another longshot. Black and white.
A negative this time, in dazzle-dark,
Smudge and pallor where we make out you and me,
The selves we struggled with and struggled out of,
Two shades who have consumed each other's fire,
Two flames in sunlight that can sear and singe,
But seem like wisps of enervated air,
After-wavers, feathery ether-shifts . . .
Yet apt still to rekindle suddenly
If we find along the way charred grass and sticks
And an old fire-fragrance lingering on,

Erotic woodsmoke, witchery, intrigue,
Leaving us none the wiser, just better primed
To speed the plough again and feed the flame.

At the Wellhead

Your songs, when you sing them with your two
    eyes closed
As you always do, are like a local road
We've known every turn of in the past –
That midge-veiled, high-hedged side-road where
    you stood
Looking and listening until a car
Would come and go and leave you lonelier
Than you had been to begin with. So, sing on,
Dear shut-eyed one, dear far-voiced veteran,

Sing yourself to where the singing comes from,
Ardent and cut off like our blind neighbour
Who played the piano all day in her bedroom.
Her notes came out to us like hoisted water
Ravelling off a bucket at the wellhead
Where next thing we'd be listening, hushed and
    awkward.

*

That blind-from-birth, sweet-voiced, withdrawn
    musician
Was like a silver vein in heavy clay.
Night water glittering in the light of day.
But also just our neighbour, Rosie Keenan.
She touched our cheeks. She let us touch her braille
In books like books wallpaper patterns came in.
Her hands were active and her eyes were full
Of open darkness and a watery shine.

She knew us by our voices. She'd say she 'saw'
Whoever or whatever. Being with her
Was intimate and helpful, like a cure
You didn't notice happening. When I read
A poem with Keenan's well in it, she said,
'I can see the sky at the bottom of it now.'

At Banagher

Then all of a sudden there appears to me
The journeyman tailor who was my antecedent:
Up on a table, cross-legged, ripping out

A garment he must recut or resew,
His lips tight back, a thread between his teeth,
Keeping his counsel always, giving none,

His eyelids steady as wrinkled horn or iron.
Self-absenting, both migrant and ensconced;
Admitted into kitchens, into clothes

His touch has the power to turn to cloth again –
All of a sudden he appears to me,
Unopen, unmendacious, unillumined.

*

So more power to him on the job there, ill at ease
Under my scrutiny in spite of years
Of being inscrutable as he threaded needles

Or matched the facings, linings, hems and seams.
He holds the needle just off centre, squinting,
And licks the thread and licks and sweeps it through,

Then takes his time to draw both ends out even,
Plucking them sharply twice. Then back to stitching.
Does he ever question what it all amounts to

Or ever will? Or care where he lays his head?
My Lord Buddha of Banagher, the way
Is opener for your being in it.

Tollund

That Sunday morning we had travelled far.
We stood a long time out in Tollund Moss:
The low ground, the swart water, the thick grass
Hallucinatory and familiar.

A path through Jutland fields. Light traffic sound.
Willow bushes; rushes; bog-fir grags
In a swept and gated farmyard; dormant quags.
And silage under wraps in its silent mound.

It could have been a still out of the bright
'Townland of Peace', that poem of dream farms
Outside all contention. The scarecrow's arms
Stood open opposite the satellite

Dish in the paddock, where a standing stone
Had been resituated and landscaped,
With tourist signs in *futhark* runic script
In Danish and in English. Things had moved on.

It could have been Mulhollandstown or Scribe.
The by-roads had their names on them in black
And white; it was user-friendly outback
Where we stood footloose, at home beyond the tribe,

More scouts than strangers, ghosts who'd walked abroad
Unfazed by light, to make a new beginning
And make a go of it, alive and sinning,
Ourselves again, free-willed again, not bad.

September 1994

Postscript

And some time make the time to drive out west
Into County Clare, along the Flaggy Shore,
In September or October, when the wind
And the light are working off each other
So that the ocean on one side is wild
With foam and glitter, and inland among stones
The surface of a slate-grey lake is lit
By the earthed lightning of a flock of swans,
Their feathers roughed and ruffling, white on white,
Their fully grown headstrong-looking heads
Tucked or cresting or busy underwater.
Useless to think you'll park and capture it
More thoroughly. You are neither here nor there,
A hurry through which known and strange things pass
As big soft buffetings come at the car sideways
And catch the heart off guard and blow it open.

from Beowulf

So. The Spear-Danes in days gone by
and the kings who ruled them had courage and greatness.
We have heard of those princes' heroic campaigns.

There was Shield Sheafson, scourge of many tribes,
a wrecker of mead-benches, rampaging among foes.
This terror of the hall-troops had come far.
A foundling to start with, he would flourish later on
as his powers waxed and his worth was proved.
In the end each clan on the outlying coasts
beyond the whale-road had to yield to him
and begin to pay tribute. That was one good king.

Afterwards a boy-child was born to Shield,
a cub in the yard, a comfort sent
by God to that nation. He knew what they had tholed,
the long times and troubles they'd come through
without a leader; so the Lord of Life,
the glorious Almighty, made this man renowned.
Shield had fathered a famous son:
Beow's name was known through the north.
And a young prince must be prudent like that,
giving freely while his father lives
so that afterwards in age when fighting starts
steadfast companions will stand by him
and hold the line. Behaviour that's admired
is the path to power among people everywhere.

Shield was still thriving when his time came
and he crossed over into the Lord's keeping.
His warrior band did what he bade them
when he laid down the law among the Danes:
they shouldered him out to the sea's flood,
the chief they revered who had long ruled them.
A ring-whorled prow rode in the harbour,
ice-clad, outbound, a craft for a prince.
They stretched their beloved lord in his boat,
laid out by the mast, amidships,
the great ring-giver. Far-fetched treasures
were piled upon him, and precious gear.
I never heard before of a ship so well furbished
with battle-tackle, bladed weapons
and coats of mail. The massed treasure
was loaded on top of him: it would travel far
on out into the ocean's sway.
They decked his body no less bountifully
with offerings than those first ones did
who cast him away when he was a child
and launched him alone out over the waves.
And they set a gold standard up
high above his head and let him drift
to wind and tide, bewailing him
and mourning their loss. No man can tell,
no wise man in hall or weathered veteran
knows for certain who salvaged that load.

Then it fell to Beow to keep the forts.
He was well regarded and ruled the Danes
for a long time after his father took leave
of his life on earth. And then his heir,
the great Halfdane, held sway

for as long as he lived, their elder and warlord.
He was four times a father, this fighter prince:
one by one they entered the world,
Heorogar, Hrothgar, the good Halga
and a daughter, I have heard, who was Onela's queen,
a balm in bed for the battle-scarred Swede.
The fortunes of war favoured Hrothgar.
Friends and kinsmen flocked to his ranks,
young followers, a force that grew
to a mighty army. So his mind turned
to hall-building: he handed down orders
for men to work on a great mead-hall
meant to be a wonder of the world for ever;
it would be his throne-room and there he would dispense
his God-given goods to young and old –
but not the common land or people's lives.
Far and wide through the world, I have heard,
orders for work to adorn that wallstead
were sent to many peoples. And soon it stood there,
finished and ready, in full view,
the hall of halls. Heorot was the name
he had settled on it, whose utterance was law.
Nor did he renege, but doled out rings
and torques at the table. The hall towered,
its gables wide and high and awaiting
a barbarous burning. That doom abided,
but in time it would come: the killer instinct
unleashed among in-laws, the blood-lust rampant.

Then a powerful demon, a prowler through the dark,
nursed a hard grievance. It harrowed him
to hear the din of the loud banquet
every day in the hall, the harp being struck

and the clear song of a skilled poet
telling with mastery of man's beginnings,
how the Almighty had made the earth
a gleaming plain girdled with waters;
in His splendour He set the sun and the moon
to be earth's lamplight, lanterns for men,
and filled the broad lap of the world
with branches and leaves; and quickened life
in every other thing that moved.

So times were pleasant for the people there
until finally one, a fiend out of hell,
began to work his evil in the world.
Grendel was the name of this grim demon
haunting the marches, marauding round the heath
and the desolate fens; he had dwelt for a time
in misery among the banished monsters,
Cain's clan, whom the Creator had outlawed
and condemned as outcasts. For the killing of Abel
the Eternal Lord had exacted a price:
Cain got no good from committing that murder
because the Almighty made him anathema
and out of the curse of his exile there sprang
ogres and elves and evil phantoms
and the giants too who strove with God
time and again until He gave them their reward.

So, after nightfall, Grendel set out
for the lofty house, to see how the Ring-Danes
were settling into it after their drink,
and there he came upon them, a company of the best
asleep from their feasting, insensible to pain
and human sorrow. Suddenly then

the God-cursed brute was creating havoc:
greedy and grim, he grabbed thirty men
from their resting places and rushed to his lair,
flushed up and inflamed from the raid,
blundering back with the butchered corpses.

Then as dawn brightened and the day broke
Grendel's powers of destruction were plain:
their wassail was over, they wept to heaven
and mourned under morning. Their mighty prince,
the storied leader, sat stricken and helpless,
humiliated by the loss of his guard,
bewildered and stunned, staring aghast
at the demon's trail, in deep distress.
He was numb with grief, but got no respite
for one night later merciless Grendel
struck again with more gruesome murders.
Malignant by nature, he never showed remorse.
It was easy then to meet with a man
shifting himself to a safer distance
to bed in the bothies, for who could be blind
to the evidence of his eyes, the obviousness
of that hall-watcher's hate? Whoever escaped
kept a weather-eye open and moved away.

So Grendel ruled in defiance of right,
one against all, until the greatest house
in the world stood empty, a deserted wallstead.
For twelve winters, seasons of woe,
the lord of the Shieldings suffered under
his load of sorrow; and so, before long,
the news was known over the whole world.
Sad lays were sung about the beset king,

the vicious raids and ravages of Grendel,
his long and unrelenting feud,
nothing but war; how he would never
parley or make peace with any Dane
nor stop his death-dealing nor pay the death-price.
No counsellor could ever expect
fair reparation from those rabid hands.
All were endangered; young and old
were hunted down by that dark death-shadow
who lurked and swooped in the long nights
on the misty moors; nobody knows
where these reavers from hell roam on their errands.

The Geat people built a pyre for Beowulf,
stacked and decked it until it stood foursquare,
hung with helmets, heavy war-shields
and shining armour, just as he had ordered.
Then his warriors laid him in the middle of it,
mourning a lord far-famed and beloved.
On a height they kindled the hugest of all
funeral fires; fumes of woodsmoke
billowed darkly up, the blaze roared
and drowned out their weeping, wind died down
and flames wrought havoc in the hot bone-house,
burning it to the core. They were disconsolate
and wailed aloud for their lord's decease.
A Geat woman too sang out in grief;
with hair bound up, she unburdened herself
of her worst fears, a wild litany
of nightmare and lament: her nation invaded,
enemies on the rampage, bodies in piles,
slavery and abasement. Heaven swallowed the smoke.

Then the Geat people began to construct
a mound on a headland, high and imposing,
a marker that sailors could see from afar,
and in ten days they had done the work.
It was their hero's memorial; what remained from the fire
they housed inside it, behind a wall
as worthy of him as their workmanship could make it.
And they buried torques in the barrow, and jewels
and a trove of such things as trespassing men
had once dared to drag from the hoard.

They let the ground keep that ancestral treasure,
gold under gravel, gone to earth,
as useless to men now as it ever was.
Then twelve warriors rode around the tomb,
chieftains' sons, champions in battle,
all of them distraught, chanting in dirges,
mourning his loss as a man and a king.
They extolled his heroic nature and exploits
and gave thanks for his greatness; which was the
        proper thing
for a man should praise a prince whom he holds dear
and cherish his memory when that moment comes
when he has to be convoyed from his bodily home.
So the Geat people, his hearth-companions,
sorrowed for the lord who had been laid low.
They said that of all the kings upon the earth
he was the man most gracious and fair-minded,
kindest to his people and keenest to win fame.

Perch

Perch on their water-perch hung in the clear Bann River
Near the clay bank in alder-dapple and waver,

Perch we called 'grunts', little flood-slubs, runty and
   ready,
I saw and I see in the river's glorified body

That is passable through, but they're bluntly holding
   the pass,
Under the water-roof, over the bottom, adoze,

Guzzling the current, against it, all muscle and slur
In the finland of perch, the fenland of alder, on air

That is water, on carpets of Bann stream, on hold
In the everything flows and steady go of the world.

Lupins

They stood. And stood for something. Just by standing.
In waiting. Unavailable. But there
For sure. Sure and unbending.
Rose-fingered dawn's and navy midnight's flower.

Seed packets to begin with, pink and azure,
Sifting lightness and small jittery promise:
Lupin spires, erotics of the future,
Lip-brush of the blue and earth's deep purchase.

O pastel turrets, pods and tapering stalks
That stood their ground for all our summer wending
And even when they blanched would never balk.
And none of this surpassed our understanding.

from Out of the Bag

All of us came in Doctor Kerlin's bag.
He'd arrive with it, disappear to the room
And by the time he'd reappear to wash

Those nosy, rosy, big, soft hands of his
In the scullery basin, its lined insides
(The colour of a spaniel's inside lug)

Were empty for all to see, the trap-sprung mouth
Unsnibbed and gaping wide. Then like a hypnotist
Unwinding us, he'd wind the instruments

Back into their lining, tie the cloth
Like an apron round itself,
Darken the door and leave

With the bag in his hand, a plump ark by the keel . . .
Until the next time came and in he'd come
In his fur-lined collar that was also spaniel-coloured

And go stooping up to the room again, a whiff
Of disinfectant, a Dutch interior gleam
Of waistcoat satin and highlights on the forceps.

Getting the water ready, that was next –
Not plumping hot, and not lukewarm, but soft,
Sud-luscious, saved for him from the rain-butt

And savoured by him afterwards, all thanks
Denied as he towelled hard and fast,
Then held his arms out suddenly behind him

To be squired and silk-lined into the camel coat.
At which point he once turned his eyes upon me,
Hyperborean, beyond-the-north-wind blue,

Two peepholes to the locked room I saw into
Every time his name was mentioned, skimmed
Milk and ice, swabbed porcelain, the white

And chill of tiles, steel hooks, chrome surgery tools
And blood dreeps in the sawdust where it thickened
At the foot of each cold wall. And overhead

The little, pendent, teat-hued infant parts
Strung neatly from a line up near the ceiling –
A toe, a foot and shin, an arm, a cock

A bit like the rosebud in his buttonhole.

4

The room I came from and the rest of us all came from
Stays pure reality where I stand alone,
Standing the passage of time, and she's asleep

In sheets put on for the doctor, wedding presents
That showed up again and again, bridal
And usual and useful at births and deaths.

Me at the bedside, incubating for real,
Peering, appearing to her as she closes
And opens her eyes, then lapses back

Into a faraway smile whose precinct of vision
I would enter every time, to assist and be asked
In that hoarsened whisper of triumph,

'And what do you think
Of the new wee baby the doctor brought for us all
When I was asleep?'

The Little Canticles of Asturias

1

And then at midnight as we started to descend
Into the burning valley of Gijon,
Into its blacks and crimsons, *in medias res*,
It was as if my own face burned again
In front of the fanned-up lip and crimson maw
Of a pile of newspapers lit long ago
One windy evening, breaking off and away
In flame-posies, small airborne fire-ships
Endangering the house-thatch and the stacks –
For we almost panicked there in the epic blaze
Of those furnaces and hot refineries
Where the night-shift worked on in their element
And we lost all hope of reading the map right
And gathered speed and cursed the hellish roads.

2

Next morning on the way to Piedras Blancas
I felt like a soul being prayed for.
I saw men cutting aftergrass with scythes,
Beehives in clover, a windlass and a shrine,
The maize like golden cargo in its hampers.
I was a pilgrim new upon the scene
Yet entering it as if it were home ground,
The Gaeltacht, say, in the nineteen-fifties,
Where I was welcome, but of small concern
To families at work in the roadside fields

Who'd watch and wave at me from their other world
As was the custom still near Piedras Blancas.

3

At San Juan de las Harenas
It was a bright day of the body.
Two rivers flowed together under sunlight.
Watercourses scored the level sand.
The sea hushed and glittered outside the bar.
And in the afternoon, gulls *in excelsis*
Bobbed and flashed on air like altar boys
With their quick turns and tapers and responses
In the great re-echoing cathedral gloom
Of distant Compostela, *stela, stela.*

Ballynahinch Lake

Godi, fanciullo mio; stato soave,
Stagion lieta è cotesta.

LEOPARDI, 'Il Sabato del Villaggio'

for Eamon Grennan

So we stopped and parked in the spring-cleaning light
Of Connemara on a Sunday morning
As a captivating brightness held and opened
And the utter mountain mirrored in the lake
Entered us like a wedge knocked sweetly home
Into core timber.
                            Not too far away
But far enough for their rumpus not to carry,
A pair of waterbirds splashed up and down
And on and on. Next thing their strong white flex
That could have been excitement or the death-throes
Turned into lift-off, big sure sweeps and dips
Above the water – no rafter-skimming souls
Translating in and out of the house of life
But air-heavers, far heavier than the air.

Yet something in us had unhoused itself
At the sight of them, so that when she bent
To turn the key she only half-turned it
And spoke, as it were, directly to the windscreen,
In profile and in thought, the wheel at arm's length,
Averring that this time, yes, it had indeed
Been useful to stop; then inclined her driver's brow
Which shook a little as the ignition fired.

The Clothes Shrine

It was a whole new sweetness
In the early days to find
Light white muslin blouses
On a see-through nylon line
Drip-drying in the bathroom
Or a nylon slip in the shine
Of its own electricity –
As if St Brigid once more
Had rigged up a ray of sun
Like the one she'd strung on air
To dry her own cloak on
(Hard-pressed Brigid, so
Unstoppably on the go) –
The damp and slump and unfair
Drag of the workaday
Made light of and got through
As usual, brilliantly.

Glanmore Eclogue

A house and ground. And your own bay tree as well
And time to yourself. You've landed on your feet.
If you can't write now, when will you ever write?

POET

A woman changed my life. Call her Augusta
Because we arrived in August, and from now on
This month's baled hay and blackberries and combines
Will spell Augusta's bounty.

MYLES

                                    Outsiders own
The country nowadays, but even so
I don't begrudge you. You're Augusta's tenant
And that's enough. She has every right,
Maybe more right than most, to her quarter acre.
She knows the big glen inside out, and everything
Meliboeus ever wrote about it,
All the tramps he met tramping the roads
And all he picked up, listening in a loft
To servant girls colloguing in the kitchen.
Talk about changed lives! Those were the days –
Land Commissions making tenants owners,
Empire taking note at last too late . . .
But now with all this money coming in

[129]

And peace being talked up, the boot's on the other foot.
First it was Meliboeus' people
Went to the wall, now it will be us.
Small farmers here are priced out of the market.

POET

Backs to the wall and empty pockets: Meliboeus
Was never happier than when he was on the road
With people on their uppers. Loneliness
Was his passport through the world. Midge-angels
On the face of water, the first drop before thunder,
A stranger on a wild night, *out in the rain falling.*
His spirit lives for me in things like that.

MYLES

Book-learning is the thing. You're a lucky man.
No stock to feed, no milking times, no tillage
Nor blisters on your hand nor weather-worries.

POET

Meliboeus would have called me 'Mr Honey'.

MYLES

Our old language that Meliboeus learnt
Has lovely songs. What about putting words
On one of them, words that the rest of us
Can understand, and singing it here and now?

POET

I have this summer song for the glen and you:

Early summer, cuckoo cuckoos,
Welcome, summer is what he sings.
Heather breathes on soft bog-pillows.
Bog-cotton bows to moorland wind.

The deer's heart skips a beat; he startles.
The sea's tide fills, it rests, it runs.
Season of the drowsy ocean.
Tufts of yellow-blossoming whins.

Bogbanks shine like ravens' wings.
The cuckoo keeps on calling *Welcome*.
The speckled fish jumps; and the strong
Warrior is up and running.

A little nippy chirpy fellow
Hits the highest note there is;
The lark sings out his clear tidings.
Summer, shimmer, perfect days.

Sonnets from Hellas

1 *Into Arcadia*

It was opulence and amen on the mountain road.
Walnuts bought on a high pass from a farmer
Who'd worked in Melbourne once and now trained water
Through a system of pipes and runnels of split reed
Known in Hellas, probably, since Hesiod –
That was the least of it. When we crossed the border
From Argos into Arcadia, and farther
Into Arcadia, a lorry load
Of apples had burst open on the road
So that for yards our tyres raunched and scrunched them
But we drove on, juiced up and fleshed and spattered,
Revelling in it. And then it was the goatherd
With his goats in the forecourt of the filling station,
Subsisting beyond eclogue and translation.

2 *Conkers*

All along the dank, sunk, rock-floored lane
To the acropolis in Sparta, we couldn't help
Tramping on burst shells and crunching down
The high-gloss horse-chestnuts. I thought of kelp
And foals' hooves, bladderwort, dubbed leather
As I bent to gather them, a hint of ordure
Coming and going off their tainted pith.
Cyclopic stone on each side of the path.
Rings of defence. Breached walls. The looted conkers
Gravid in my satchel, swinging nicely.
Then a daylight moon appeared behind Dimitri
As he sketched and squared his shoulders like a centaur's
And nodded, nodded, nodded towards the spouses,
Heard but not seen behind much thick acanthus.

3 Pylos

Barbounia schooled below the balcony –
Shadows on shelving sand in sandy Pylos.
Wave-clip and flirt, tide-slap and flop and flow:
I woke to the world there like Telemachos,
Young again in the whitewashed light of morning
That flashed on the ceiling like an early warning
From myself to be more myself in the mast-bending
Marine breeze, to key the understanding
To that image of the bow strung as a lyre
Robert Fitzgerald spoke of: Harvard Nestor,
Sponsor and host, translator of all Homer,
His wasted face in profile, ceiling-staring
As he schooled me in the course, not yet past caring,
Scanning the offing. Far-seeing shadower.

4 The Augean Stables

My favourite bas-relief: Athene showing
Heracles where to broach the river bank
With a nod of her high helmet, her staff sunk
In the exact spot, the Alpheus flowing
Out of its course into the deep dung strata
Of King Augeas' reeking yard and stables.
Sweet dissolutions from the water tables,
Blocked doors and packed floors deluging like gutters . . .
And it was there in Olympia, down among green willows,
The lustral wash and run of river shallows,
That we heard of Sean Brown's murder in the grounds
Of Bellaghy GAA Club. And imagined
Hose-water smashing hard back off the asphalt
In the car park where his athlete's blood ran cold.

5 *Castalian Spring*

Thunderface. Not Zeus's ire, but hers
Refusing entry, and mine mounting from it.
This one thing I had vowed: to drink the waters
Of the Castalian Spring, to arrogate
That much to myself and be the poet
Under the god Apollo's giddy cliff –
But the inner water sanctum was roped off
When we arrived. Well then, to hell with that,
And to hell with all who'd stop me, thunderface!
So up the steps then, into the sandstone grottoes,
The seeps and dreeps, the shallow pools, the mosses,
Come from beyond, and come far, with this useless
Anger draining away, on terraces
Where I bowed and mouthed in sweetness and defiance.

6 Desfina

Mount Parnassus placid on the skyline:
Slieve na mBard, Knock Filiocht, Ben Duan.
We gaelicized new names for Poetry Hill
As we wolfed down horta, tarama and houmos
At sunset in the farmyard, drinking ouzos,
Pretending not to hear the Delphic squeal
Of the streel-haired *cailleach* in the scullery.
Then it was time to head into Desfina
To allow them to sedate her. And so retsina,
Anchovies, squid, dolmades, french fries even.
My head was light, I was hyper, boozed, borean
As we bowled back down towards the olive plain,
Siren-tyred and manic on the horn
Round hairpin bends looped like boustrophedon.

Vitruviana

for Felim Egan

In the deep pool at Portstewart, I waded in
Up to the chest, then stood there half-suspended
Like Vitruvian man, both legs wide apart,
Both arms out buoyant to the fingertips,
Oxter-cogged on water.
                              My head was light,
My backbone plumb, my boy-nipples bisected
And tickled by the steel-zip cold meniscus.

*

On the hard scrabble of the junior football pitch
Where Leo Day, the college 'drillie', bounced
And counted and kept us all in line
In front of the wooden horse – '*One! Two! In! Out!*' –
We upped and downed and scissored arms and legs
And spread ourselves on the wind's cross, felt our palms
As tautly strung as Francis of Assisi's
In Giotto's mural, where angelic neon
Zaps the ping-palmed saint with the stigmata.

*

On Sandymount Strand I can connect
Some bits and pieces. My seaside whirligig.
The cardinal points. The grey matter of sand
And sky. And a light that is down to earth
Beginning to fan out and open up.

Audenesque

in memory of Joseph Brodsky

Joseph, yes, you know the beat.
Wystan Auden's metric feet
Marched to it, unstressed and stressed,
Laying William Yeats to rest.

Therefore, Joseph, on this day,
Yeats's anniversary,
(Double-crossed and death-marched date,
January twenty-eight),

Its measured ways I tread again
Quatrain by constrained quatrain,
Meting grief and reason out
As you said a poem ought.

Trochee, trochee, falling: thus
Grief and metre order us.
Repetition is the rule,
Spins on lines we learnt at school.

Repetition, too, of cold
In the poet and the world,
Dublin Airport locked in frost,
Rigor mortis in your breast.

Ice no axe or book will break,
No Horatian ode unlock,
No poetic foot imprint,
Quatrain shift or couplet dint,

Ice of Archangelic strength,
Ice of this hard two-faced month,
Ice like Dante's in deep hell
Makes your heart a frozen well.

Pepper vodka you produced
Once in Western Massachusetts
With the reading due to start
Warmed my spirits and my heart

But no vodka, cold or hot,
Aquavit or uisquebaugh
Brings the blood back to your cheeks
Or the colour to your jokes,

Politically incorrect
Jokes involving sex and sect,
Everything against the grain,
Drinking, smoking like a train.

In a train in Finland we
Talked last summer happily,
Swapping manuscripts and quips,
Both of us like cracking whips

Sharpened up and making free,
Heading west for Tampere
(West that meant for you, of course,
Lenin's train-trip in reverse).

Nevermore that wild speed-read,
Nevermore your tilted head

Like a deck where mind took off
With a mind-flash and a laugh,

Nevermore that rush to pun
Or to hurry through all yon
Jammed enjambements piling up
As you went above the top,

Nose in air, foot to the floor,
Revving English like a car
You hijacked when you robbed its bank
(Russian was your reserve tank).

Worshipped language can't undo
Damage time has done to you:
Even your peremptory trust
In words alone here bites the dust.

Dust-cakes, still – see *Gilgamesh* –
Feed the dead. So be their guest.
Do again what Auden said
Good poets do: bite, break their bread.

To the Shade of Zbigniew Herbert

You were one of those from the back of the north wind
Whom Apollo favoured and would keep going back to
In the winter season. And among your people you
Remained his herald whenever he'd departed
And the land was silent and summer's promise thwarted.
You learnt the lyre from him and kept it tuned.

Bodies and Souls

1 *In the Afterlife*

It will be like following Jim Logue, the caretaker,
As he goes to sweep our hair off that classroom floor
Where the school barber set up once a fortnight,
Falling into step as he does his rounds,
Glimmerman of dorms and silent landings,
Of the refectory with its solid, crest-marked delph,
The ground-floor corridor, the laundry pile
And boots tagged for the cobbler. Was that your name
On a label? Were you a body or a soul?

2 *Nights of '57*

It wasn't asphodel but mown grass
We practised on each night after night prayers
When we lapped the college front lawn in bare feet,

Heel-bone and heart-thud, open-mouthed for summer.
The older I get, the quicker and the closer
I hear those labouring breaths and feel the coolth.

3 *The Bereaved*

Set apart. First out down the aisle
Like brides. Or those boys who were permitted
To leave the study early for music practice –
Privileged and unenvied, left alone

In the four bare walls to face the exercise,
Eyes shut, shoulders straight back, cold hands out
Above the keys. And then the savagery
Of the piano music's music going wrong.

from Electric Light

Lisp and relapse. Eddy of sybilline English.
Splashes between a ship and dock, to which,
Animula, I would come alive in time

As ferries churned and turned down Belfast Lough
Towards the brow-to-glass transport of a morning train,
The very 'there-you-are-and-where-are-you?'

Of poetry itself. Backs of houses
Like the back of hers, meat-safes and mangles
In the railway-facing yards of fleeting England,

An allotment scarecrow among patted rigs,
Then a town-edge soccer pitch, the groin of distance,
Fields of grain like the Field of the Cloth of Gold.

To Southwark too I came,
From tube-mouth into sunlight,
Moyola-breath by Thames's 'straunge stronde'.

A Shiver

The way you had to stand to swing the sledge,
Your two knees locked, your lower back shock-fast
As shields in a *testudo*, spine and waist
A pivot for the tight-braced, tilting rib-cage;
The way its iron head planted the sledge
Unyieldingly as a club-footed last;
The way you had to heft and then half-rest
Its gathered force like a long-nursed rage
About to be let fly: does it do you good
To have known it in your bones, directable,
Withholdable at will,
A first blow that could make air of a wall,
A last one so unanswerably landed
The staked earth quailed and shivered in the handle?

Anahorish 1944

'We were killing pigs when the Americans arrived.
A Tuesday morning, sunlight and gutter-blood
Outside the slaughterhouse. From the main road
They would have heard the squealing,
Then heard it stop and had a view of us
In our gloves and aprons coming down the hill.
Two lines of them, guns on their shoulders, marching.
Armoured cars and tanks and open jeeps.
Sunburnt hands and arms. Unknown, unnamed,
Hosting for Normandy.
           Not that we knew then
Where they were headed, standing there like youngsters
As they tossed us gum and tubes of coloured sweets.'

Anything Can Happen

after Horace, Odes, *1, 34*

Anything can happen. You know how Jupiter
Will mostly wait for clouds to gather head
Before he hurls the lightning? Well, just now
He galloped his thunder cart and his horses

Across a clear blue sky. It shook the earth
And the clogged underearth, the River Styx,
The winding streams, the Atlantic shore itself.
Anything can happen, the tallest towers

Be overturned, those in high places daunted,
Those overlooked regarded. Stropped-beak Fortune
Swoops, making the air gasp, tearing the crest off one,
Setting it down bleeding on the next.

Ground gives. The heaven's weight
Lifts up off Atlas like a kettle-lid.
Capstones shift, nothing resettles right.
Telluric ash and fire-spores boil away.

District and Circle

Tunes from a tin whistle underground
Curled up a corridor I'd be walking down
To where I knew I was always going to find
My watcher on the tiles, cap by his side,
His fingers perked, his two eyes eyeing me
In an unaccusing look I'd not avoid,
Or not just yet, since both were out to see
For ourselves.
                    As the music larked and capered
I'd trigger and untrigger a hot coin
Held at the ready, but now my gaze was lowered
For was our traffic not in recognition?
Accorded passage, I would re-pocket and nod,
And he, still eyeing me, would also nod.

                              *

Posted, eyes front, along the dreamy ramparts
Of escalators ascending and descending
To a monotonous slight rocking in the works,
We were moved along, upstanding.
Elsewhere, underneath, an engine powered,
Rumbled, quickened, evened, quieted.
The white tiles gleamed. In passages that flowed
With draughts from cooler tunnels, I missed the light
Of all-overing, long since mysterious day,
Parks at lunchtime where the sunners lay
On body-heated mown grass regardless,
A resurrection scene minutes before
The resurrection, habitués
Of their garden of delights, of staggered summer.

*

Another level down, the platform thronged.
I re-entered the safety of numbers,
A crowd half straggle-ravelled and half strung
Like a human chain, the pushy newcomers
Jostling and purling underneath the vault,
On their marks to be first through the doors,
Street-loud, then succumbing to herd-quiet . . .
Had I betrayed or not, myself or him?
Always new to me, always familiar,
This unrepentant, now repentant turn
As I stood waiting, glad of a first tremor,
Then caught up in the now-or-never whelm
Of one and all the full length of the train.

*

Stepping on to it across the gap,
On to the carriage metal, I reached to grab
The stubby black roof-wort and take my stand
From planted ball of heel to heel of hand
As sweet traction and heavy down-slump stayed me.
I was on my way, well girded, yet on edge,
Spot-rooted, buoyed, aloof,
Listening to the dwindling noises off,
My back to the unclosed door, the platform empty;
And wished it could have lasted,
That long between-times pause before the budge
And glaze-over, when any forwardness
Was unwelcome and bodies readjusted,
Blindsided to themselves and other bodies.

So deeper into it, crowd-swept, strap-hanging,
My lofted arm a-swivel like a flail,
My father's glazed face in my own waning
And craning . . .
                    Again the growl
Of shutting doors, the jolt and one-off treble
Of iron on iron, then a long centrifugal
Haulage of speed through every dragging socket.

And so by night and day to be transported
Through galleried earth with them, the only relict
Of all that I belonged to, hurtled forward,
Reflecting in a window mirror-backed
By blasted weeping rock-walls.
                    Flicker-lit.

Wordsworth's Skates

Star in the window.
                    Slate scrape.
                                Bird or branch?
Or the whet and scud of steel on placid ice?

Not the bootless runners lying toppled
In dust in a display case,
Their bindings perished,

But the reel of them on frozen Windermere
As he flashed from the clutch of earth along its curve
And left it scored.

Found Prose

1 *The Lagans Road*

The Lagans Road ran for about three quarters of a mile across an area of wetlands. It was one of those narrow country roads with weeds in the middle, grass verges and high hedges on either side, and all around it marsh and rushes and little shrubs and birch trees. For a minute or two every day, therefore, you were in the wilderness, but on the first morning I went to school it was as if the queen of elfland was leading me away. The McNicholls were neighbours and Philomena McNicholl had been put in charge of me during those first days. Ginger hair, freckled face, green gymfrock – a fey, if ever there was one. I remember my first sight of the school, a couple of low-set Nissen huts raising their corrugated backs above the hedges. From about a quarter of a mile away I could see youngsters running about in the road in front of the buildings and hear shouting in the playground. Years later, when I read an account of how the Indians of the Pacific Northwest foresaw their arrival in the land of the dead – coming along a forest path where other travellers' cast-offs lay scattered on the bushes, hearing voices laughing and calling, knowing there was a life in the clearing up ahead that would be familiar, but feeling at the same time lost and homesick – it struck me I had already experienced that kind of arrival. Next thing in the porch I was faced with rows of coathooks nailed up at different heights along the wall, so that everyone in the different classes could reach them, everyone had a place to hang overcoat or scarf and proceed to the strange room, where our names were new in the rollbook and would soon be called.

2 Tall Dames

Even though we called them 'the gypsies', we knew that gypsies were properly another race. They inhabited the land of eros, glimpsed occasionally when the circus rolled into a field and a fortune-teller, swathed in her silks and beads, inclined to us from the back door of a caravan. The people we called 'the gypsies' we would now call travellers, although at that time in that place 'tinker' was an honourable term, signifying tin-smiths, white-smiths, pony-keepers, regulars on the doorstep, squatters on the long acre. Marvellous upfront women in unerotic woollen shawls, woven in big tartan patterns of tan and mossy green, their baskets full of dyed wooden flowers, their speech cadenced to beg and keep begging with all the stamina of a cantor. Walking the roads in ones and twos, children on their arms or at their heels. Squaws of the ditchback, in step with Yeats's 'tall dames' walking in Avalon.

You encountered them in broad daylight, going about their usual business, yet there was always a feeling that they were coming towards you out of storytime. One of the menfolk on the road with a bit of a halter, you on your way to school, he with a smell of woodsmoke off him, asking if you'd seen an old horse anywhere behind the hedges. The stillness of the low tarpaulin tent as you approached and passed, the green wood in the fire spitting under a pot slung from a tripod. Every time they landed in the district, there was an extra-ness in the air, as if a gate had been left open in the usual life, as if something might get in or get out.

3 Boarders

There's no heat in the bus, but the engine's running and up where a destination should be showing it just says PRIVATE, so it must be ours. We're back in the days of peaked caps and braid piping, drivers mounting steps as ominously as hangmen, conductors with plump bags of coin, the ticket punch a-dangle on its chain. But this is a special bus, so there'll be no tickets, no conductor and no fare collection until the load is full.

The stops are the same as every other time, clusters of us with suitcases assembled in shop doorways or at the appointed crossroads, the old bus getting up speed wherever the going's good, but now she's changing down on Glenshane Pass. The higher she goes, the heavier she pulls, and yet there's no real hurry. Let the driver keep doing battle with the gear-stick, let his revs and double-clutchings drag the heart, anything to put off that last stop when he slows down at the summit and turns and seems about to take us back. Instead of which he halts, pulls on the handbrake, gives us time to settle, then switches off.

When we start again, the full lock of the steering will be held, the labour of cut and spin leave tyre-marks in the gravel, the known country fall away behind us. But for the moment it's altogether quiet, the whole bus shakes as he bangs the cabin door shut, comes round the side and in to lift the money. Unfamiliar, uninvolved, almost, it seems, angered, he deals with us one by one, as one by one we go farther into ourselves, wishing we were him

on the journey back, flailing downhill with the windows
all lit up, empty and faster and angrier bend after bend.

The Lift

A first green braird: the hawthorn half in leaf.
Her funeral filled the road
And could have stepped from some old photograph

Of a Breton *pardon*, remote
Familiar women and men in caps
Walking four abreast, soon falling quiet.

Then came the throttle and articulated whops
Of a helicopter crossing, and afterwards
Awareness of the sound of our own footsteps,

Of open air, and the life behind those words
'Open' and 'air'. I remembered her aghast,
Foetal, shaking, sweating, shrunk, wet-haired,

A beaten breath, a misting mask, the flash
Of one wild glance, like ghost surveillance
From behind a gleam of helicopter glass.

A lifetime, then the deathtime: reticence
Keeping us together when together,
All declaration deemed outspokenness.

Favourite aunt, good sister, faithful daughter,
Delicate since childhood, tough alloy
Of disapproval, kindness and *hauteur*,

She took the risk, at last, of certain joys –
Her birdtable and jubilating birds,
The 'fashion' in her wardrobe and her tallboy.

Weather, in the end, would say our say.
Reprise of griefs in summer's clearest mornings,
Children's deaths in snowdrops and the may,

Whole requiems at the sight of plants and gardens . . .
They bore her lightly on the bier. Four women,
Four friends – she would have called them girls –
    stepped in

And claimed the final lift beneath the hawthorn.

Nonce Words

The road taken
to bypass Cavan
took me west,
(a sign mistaken)
so at Derrylin
I turned east.

Sun on ice,
white floss
on reed and bush,
the bridge-iron cast
in an Advent silence
I drove across,

then pulled in,
parked, and sat
breathing mist
on the windscreen.
Requiescat . . .
I got out

well happed up,
stood at the frozen
shore gazing
at rimed horizon,
my first stop
like this in years.

And blessed myself
in the name of the nonce
and happenstance,
the *Who knows*
and *What nexts*
and *So be its.*

Stern

in memory of Ted Hughes

'And what was it like,' I asked him,
'Meeting Eliot?'
                    'When he looked at you,'
He said, 'it was like standing on a quay
Watching the prow of the *Queen Mary*
Come towards you, very slowly.'

                    Now it seems
I'm standing on a pierhead watching him
All the while watching me as he rows out
And a wooden end-stopped stern
Labours and shimmers and dips,
Making no real headway.

from Out of This World

in memory of Czeslaw Milosz

1 *'Like everybody else . . .'*

'Like everybody else, I bowed my head
during the consecration of the bread and wine,
lifted my eyes to the raised host and raised chalice,
believed (whatever it means) that a change occurred.

I went to the altar rails and received the mystery
on my tongue, returned to my place, shut my eyes fast,
made
an act of thanksgiving, opened my eyes and felt
time starting up again.
                              There was never a scene
when I had it out with myself or with another.
The loss occurred off-stage. And yet I cannot
disavow words like "thanksgiving" or "host"
or "communion bread". They have an undying
tremor and draw, like well water far down.'

In Iowa

In Iowa once, among the Mennonites
In a slathering blizzard, conveyed all afternoon
Through sleet-glit pelting hard against the windscreen
And a wiper's strong absolving slumps and flits,

I saw, abandoned in the open gap
Of a field where wilted corn stalks flagged the snow,
A mowing machine. Snow brimmed its iron seat,
Heaped each spoked wheel with a thick white brow

And took the shine off oil in the black-toothed gears.
Verily I came forth from that wilderness
As one unbaptized who had known darkness
At the third hour and the veil in tatters.

In Iowa once. In the slush and rush and hiss
Not of parted but as of rising waters.

Höfn

The three-tongued glacier has begun to melt.
What will we do, they ask, when boulder-milt
Comes wallowing across the delta flats

And the miles-deep shag-ice makes its move?
I saw it, ridged and rock-set, from above,
Undead grey-gristed earth-pelt, aeon-scruff,

And feared its coldness that still seemed enough
To iceblock the plane window dimmed with breath,
Deepfreeze the seep of adamantine tilth

And every warm, mouthwatering word of mouth.

The Tollund Man in Springtime

Into your virtual city I'll have passed
Unregistered by scans, screens, hidden eyes,
Lapping myself in time, an absorbed face
Coming and going, neither god nor ghost,
Not at odds or at one, but simply lost
To you and yours, out under seeding grass
And trickles of kesh water, sphagnum moss,
Dead bracken on the spreadfield, red as rust.
I reawoke to revel in the spirit
They strengthened when they chose to put me down
For their own good. And to a sixth-sensed threat:
Panicked snipe offshooting into twilight,
Then going awry, larks quietened in the sun,
Clear alteration in the bog-pooled rain.

*

Scone of peat, composite bog-dough
They trampled like a muddy vintage, then
Slabbed and spread and turned to dry in sun –
Though never kindling-dry the whole way through –
A dead-weight, slow-burn lukewarmth in the flue,
Ashless, flameless, its very smoke a sullen
Waft of swamp-breath . . . And me, so long unrisen,
I knew that same dead weight in joint and sinew
Until a spade-plate slid and soughed and plied
At my buried ear, and the levered sod
Got lifted up; then once I felt the air
I was like turned turf in the breath of God,
Bog-bodied on the sixth day, brown and bare,
And on the last, all told, unatrophied.

My heavy head. Bronze-buffed. Ear to the ground.
My eye at turf level. Its snailskin lid.
My cushioned cheek and brow. My phantom hand
And arm and leg and shoulder that felt pillowed
As fleshily as when the bog pith weighed
To mould me to itself and it to me
Between when I was buried and unburied.
Between what happened and was meant to be.
On show for years while all that lay in wait
Still waited. Disembodied. Far renowned.
Faith placed in me, me faithless as a stone
The harrow turned up when the crop was sown.
Out in the Danish night I'd hear soft wind
And remember moony water in a rut.

*

'The soul exceeds its circumstances.' Yes.
History not to be granted the last word
Or the first claim . . . In the end I gathered
From the display-case peat my staying powers,
Told my webbed wrists to be like silver birches,
My old uncallused hands to be young sward,
The spade-cut skin to heal, and got restored
By telling myself this. Late as it was,
The early bird still sang, the meadow hay
Still buttercupped and daisied, sky was new.
I smelled the air, exhaust fumes, silage reek,
Heard from my heather bed the thickened traffic
Swarm at a roundabout five fields away
And transatlantic flights stacked in the blue.

Cattle out in rain, their knowledgeable
Solid standing and readiness to wait,
These I learned from. My study was the wet,
My head as washy as a head of kale,
Shedding water like the flanks and tail
Of every dumb beast sunk above the cloot
In trampled gaps, bringing their heavyweight
Silence to bear on nosed-at sludge and puddle.
Of another world, unlearnable, and so
To be lived by, whatever it was I knew
Came back to me. Newfound contrariness.
In check-out lines, at cash-points, in those queues
Of wired, far-faced smilers, I stood off,
Bulrush, head in air, far from its lough.

*

Through every check and scan I carried with me
A bunch of Tollund rushes – roots and all –
Bagged in their own bog-damp. In an old stairwell
Broom cupboard where I had hoped they'd stay
Damp until transplanted, they went musty.
Every green-skinned stalk turned friable,
The drowned-mouse fibres withered and the whole
Limp, soggy cluster lost its frank bouquet
Of weed leaf and turf mould. Dust in my palm
And in my nostrils dust, should I shake it off
Or mix it in with spit in pollen's name
And my own? As a man would, cutting turf,
I straightened, spat on my hands, felt benefit
And spirited myself into the street.

Planting the Alder

For the bark, dulled argent, roundly wrapped
And pigeon-collared.

For the splitter-splatter, guttering
Rain-flirt leaves.

For the snub and clot of the first green cones,
Smelted emerald, chlorophyll.

For the scut and scat of cones in winter,
So rattle-skinned, so fossil-brittle.

For the alder-wood, flame-red when torn
Branch from branch.

But mostly for the swinging locks
Of yellow catkins,

Plant it, plant it,
Streel-head in the rain.

Tate's Avenue

Not the brown and fawn car rug, that first one
Spread on sand by the sea but breathing land-breaths,
Its vestal folds unfolded, its comfort zone
Edged with a fringe of sepia-coloured wool tails.

Not the one scraggy with crusts and eggshells
And olive stones and cheese and salami rinds
Laid out by the torrents of the Guadalquivir
Where we got drunk before the corrida.

Instead, again, it's locked-park Sunday Belfast,
A walled back yard, the dust-bins high and silent
As a page is turned, a finger twirls warm hair
And nothing gives on the rug or the ground beneath it.

I lay at my length and felt the lumpy earth,
Keen-sensed more than ever through discomfort,
But never shifted off the plaid square once.
When we moved I had your measure and you had mine.

Fiddleheads

Fiddlehead ferns are a delicacy where? Japan? Estonia?
Ireland long ago?

I say Japan because when I think of those delicious
things I think of my friend Toraiwa, and the surprise I
felt when he asked me about the erotic. He said it
belonged in poetry and he wanted more of it.

So here they are, Toraiwa, frilled, infolded, tenderized,
in a little steaming basket, just for you.

Quitting Time

The hosed-down chamfered concrete pleases him.
He'll wait a while before he kills the light
On the cleaned-up yard, its pails and farrowing crate,
And the cast-iron pump immobile as a herm
Upstanding elsewhere, in another time.
More and more this last look at the wet
Shine of the place is what means most to him –
And to repeat the phrase, 'My head is light',
Because it often is as he reaches back
And switches off, a home-based man at home
In the end with little. Except this same
Night after nightness, redding up the work,
The song of a tubular steel gate in the dark
As he pulls it to and starts his uphill trek.

The Blackbird of Glanmore

On the grass when I arrive,
Filling the stillness with life,
But ready to scare off
At the very first wrong move.
In the ivy when I leave.

It's you, blackbird, I love.

I park, pause, take heed.
Breathe. Just breathe and sit
And lines I once translated
Come back: 'I want away
To the house of death, to my father

Under the low clay roof.'

And I think of one gone to him,
A little stillness dancer –
Haunter-son, lost brother –
Cavorting through the yard,
So glad to see me home,

My homesick first term over.

And think of a neighbour's words
Long after the accident:
'Yon bird on the shed roof,
Up on the ridge for weeks –
I said nothing at the time

But I never liked yon bird.'

The automatic lock
Clunks shut, the blackbird's panic
Is shortlived, for a second
I've a bird's eye view of myself,
A shadow on raked gravel

In front of my house of life.

Hedge-hop, I am absolute
For you, your ready talkback,
Your each stand-offish comeback,
Your picky, nervy goldbeak –
On the grass when I arrive,

In the ivy when I leave.

'Had I not been awake'

Had I not been awake I would have missed it,
A wind that rose and whirled until the roof
Pattered with quick leaves off the sycamore

And got me up, the whole of me a-patter,
Alive and ticking like an electric fence:
Had I not been awake I would have missed it,

It came and went so unexpectedly
And almost it seemed dangerously,
Returning like an animal to the house,

A courier blast that there and then
Lapsed ordinary. But not ever
After. And not now.

Album

Now the oil-fired heating boiler comes to life
Abruptly, drowsily, like the timed collapse
Of a sawn down tree, I imagine them

In summer season, as it must have been,
And the place, it dawns on me,
Could have been Grove Hill before the oaks were cut,

Where I'd often stand with them on airy Sundays
Shin-deep in hilltop bluebells, looking out
At Magherafelt's four spires in the distance.

Too late, alas, now for the apt quotation
About a love that's proved by steady gazing
Not at each other but in the same direction.

II

Quercus, the oak. And *Quaerite*, Seek ye.
Among green leaves and acorns in mosaic
(Our college arms surmounted by *columba*,

Dove of the church, of Derry's sainted grove)
The footworn motto stayed indelible:
Seek ye first the Kingdom . . . Fair and square

I stood on in the Junior House hallway
A grey eye will look back
Seeing them as a couple, I now see,

For the first time, all the more together
For having had to turn and walk away, as close
In the leaving (or closer) as in the getting.

III

It's winter at the seaside where they've gone
For the wedding meal. And I am at the table,
Uninvited, ineluctable.

A skirl of gulls. A smell of cooking fish.
Plump dormant silver. Stranded silence. Tears.
Their bibbed waitress unlids a clinking dish

And leaves them to it, under chandeliers.
And to all the anniversaries of this
They are not ever going to observe

Or mention even in the years to come.
And now the man who drove them here will drive
Them back, and by evening we'll be home.

IV

Were I to have embraced him anywhere
It would have been on the riverbank
That summer before college, him in his prime,

Me at the time not thinking how he must
Keep coming with me because I'd soon be leaving.
That should have been the first, but it didn't happen.

The second did, at New Ferry one night
When he was very drunk and needed help
To do up trouser buttons. And the third

Was on the landing during his last week,
Helping him to the bathroom, my right arm
Taking the webby weight of his underarm.

V

It took a grandson to do it properly,
To rush him in the armchair
With a snatch raid on his neck,

Proving him thus vulnerable to delight,
Coming as great proofs often come
Of a sudden, one-off, then the steady dawning

Of whatever *erat demonstrandum*.
Just as a moment back a son's three tries
At an embrace in Elysium

Swam up into my very arms, and in and out
Of the Latin stem itself, the phantom
Verus that has slipped from 'very'.

The Conway Stewart

'Medium', 14-carat nib,
Three gold bands in the clip-on screw-top,
In the mottled barrel a spatulate, thin

Pump-action lever
The shopkeeper
Demonstrated,

The nib uncapped,
Treating it to its first deep snorkel
In a newly opened ink-bottle,

Guttery, snottery,
Letting it rest then at an angle
To ingest,

Giving us time
To look together and away
From our parting, due that evening,

To my longhand
'Dear'
To them, next day.

Uncoupled

I

Who is this coming to the ash-pit
Walking tall, as if in a procession,
Bearing in front of her a slender pan

Withdrawn just now from underneath
The firebox, weighty, full to the brim
With whitish dust and flakes still sparking hot

That the wind is blowing into her apron bib,
Into her mouth and eyes while she proceeds
Unwavering, keeping her burden horizontal still,

Hands in a tight, sore grip round the metal knob,
Proceeds until we have lost sight of her
Where the worn path turns behind the henhouse.

II

Who is this, not much higher than the cattle,
Working his way towards me through the pen,
His ashplant in one hand

Lifted and pointing, a stick of keel
In the other, calling to where I'm perched
On top of a shaky gate,

Waving and calling something I cannot hear
With all the lowing and roaring, lorries revving
At the far end of the yard, the dealers

Shouting among themselves, and now to him
So that his eyes leave mine and I know
The pain of loss before I know the term.

The Butts

His suits hung in the wardrobe, broad
And short
And slightly bandy-sleeved,

Flattened back
Against themselves,
A bit stand-offish.

Stale smoke and oxter-sweat
Came at you in a stirred-up brew
When you reached in,

A whole rake of thornproof and blue serge
Swung heavily
Like waterweed disturbed. I sniffed

Tonic unfreshness,
Then delved past flap and lining
For the forbidden handfuls.

But a kind of empty-handedness
Transpired . . . Out of suit-cloth
Pressed against my face,

Out of those layered stuffs
That surged and gave,
Out of the cold smooth pocket-lining

Nothing but chaff cocoons,
A paperiness not known again
Until the last days came

And we must learn to reach well in beneath
Each meagre armpit
To lift and sponge him,

One on either side,
Feeling his lightness,
Having to dab and work

Closer than anybody liked
But having, for all that,
To keep working.

Chanson d'Aventure

Love's mysteries in souls do grow,
But yet the body is his book.

I

Strapped on, wheeled out, forklifted, locked
In position for the drive,
Bone-shaken, bumped at speed,

The nurse a passenger in front, you ensconced
In her vacated corner seat, me flat on my back –
Our postures all the journey still the same,

Everything and nothing spoken,
Our eyebeams threaded laser-fast, no transport
Ever like it until then, in the sunlit cold

Of a Sunday morning ambulance
When we might, O my love, have quoted Donne
On love on hold, body and soul apart.

Apart: the very word is like a bell
That the sexton Malachy Boyle outrolled
In illo tempore in Bellaghy

Or the one I tolled in Derry in my turn
As college bellman, the haul of it there still
In the heel of my once capable

Warm hand, hand that I could not feel you lift
And lag in yours throughout that journey
When it lay flop-heavy as a bellpull

And we careered at speed through Dungloe,
Glendoan, our gaze ecstatic and bisected
By a hooked-up drip-feed to the cannula.

III

The charioteer at Delphi holds his own,
His six horses and chariot gone,
His left hand lopped

From a wrist protruding like an open spout,
Bronze reins astream in his right, his gaze ahead
Empty as the space where the team should be,

His eyes-front, straight-backed posture like my own
Doing physio in the corridor, holding up
As if once more I'd found myself in step

Between two shafts, another's hand on mine,
Each slither of the share, each stone it hit
Registered like a pulse in the timbered grips.

Miracle

Not the one who takes up his bed and walks
But the ones who have known him all along
And carry him in –

Their shoulders numb, the ache and stoop deeplocked
In their backs, the stretcher handles
Slippery with sweat. And no let-up

Until he's strapped on tight, made tiltable
And raised to the tiled roof, then lowered for healing.
Be mindful of them as they stand and wait

For the burn of the paid-out ropes to cool,
Their slight lightheadedness and incredulity
To pass, those ones who had known him all along.

Human Chain

for Terence Brown

Seeing the bags of meal passed hand to hand
In close-up by the aid workers, and soldiers
Firing over the mob, I was braced again

With a grip on two sack corners,
Two packed wads of grain I'd worked to lugs
To give me purchase, ready for the heave –

The eye-to-eye, one-two, one-two upswing
On to the trailer, then the stoop and drag and drain
Of the next lift. Nothing surpassed

That quick unburdening, backbreak's truest payback,
A letting go which will not come again.
Or it will, once. And for all.

The Baler

All day the clunk of a baler
Ongoing, cardiac-dull,
So taken for granted

It was evening before I came to
To what I was hearing
And missing: summer's richest hours

As they had been to begin with,
Fork-lifted, sweated-through
And nearly rewarded enough

By the giddied-up race of a tractor
At the end of the day
Last-lapping a hayfield.

But what I also remembered
As woodpigeons sued at the edge
Of thirty gleaned acres

And I stood inhaling the cool
In a dusk eldorado
Of mighty cylindrical bales

Was Derek Hill's saying,
The last time he sat at our table,
He could bear no longer to watch

The sun going down
And asking please to be put
With his back to the window.

Eelworks

I

To win the hand of the princess
What tasks the youngest son
Had to perform!

For me, the first to come a-courting
In the fish factor's house,
It was to eat with them

An eel supper.

II

Cut of diesel oil in evening air,
Tractor engines in the clinker-built
Deep-bellied boats,

Landlubbers' craft,
Heavy in water
As a cow down in a drain,

The men straight-backed,
Standing firm
At stern and bow –

Horse-and-cart men, really,
Glad when the adze-dressed keel
Cleaved to the mud.

Rum-and-peppermint men too
At the counter later on
In her father's pub.

III

That skin Alfie Kirkwood wore
At school, sweaty-lustrous, supple

And bisected into tails
For the tying of itself around itself –

For strength, according to Alfie.
Who would ease his lapped wrist

From the flap-mouthed cuff
Of a jerkin rank with eel oil,

The abounding reek of it
Among our summer desks

My first encounter with the up close
That had to be put up with.

IV

Sweaty-lustrous too
The butt of the freckled
Elderberry shoot

I made a rod of,
A-fluster when I felt
Not tugging but a trailing

On the line, not the utter
Flip-stream frolic-fish
But a foot-long

Slither of a fellow,
A young eel, greasy grey
And rightly wriggle-spined,

Not yet the blueblack
Slick-backed waterwork
I'd live to reckon with,

My old familiar
Pearl-purl
Selkie-streaker.

V

'That tree,' said Walter de la Mare
(Summer in his rare, recorded voice
So I could imagine

A lawn beyond French windows
And downs in the middle distance)
'That tree, saw it once

Struck by lightning . . . The bark –'
In his accent the *ba-aak* –
'The bark came off it

Like a girl taking off her petticoat.'
White linen *éblouissante*
In a breath of air,

Sylph-flash made flesh,
Eelwork, sea-salt and dish cloth
Getting a first hold,

Then purchase for the thumb nail
And the thumb
Under a v-nick in the neck,

The skinpeel drawing down
Like silk
At a practised touch.

VI

On the hoarding and the signposts
'Lough Neagh Fishermen's Co-operative',

But ever on our lips and at the weir
'The eelworks'.

The Riverbank Field

after Virgil, Aeneid, VI, 704–15, 748–51

Ask me to translate what Loeb gives as
'In a retired vale . . . a sequestered grove'
And I'll confound the Lethe in Moyola

By coming through Back Park down from Grove Hill
Across Long Rigs on to the riverbank –
Which way, by happy chance, will take me past

The *domos placidas*, 'those peaceful homes'
Of Upper Broagh. Moths then on evening water
It would have to be, not bees in sunlight,

Midge veils instead of lily beds; but *stet*
To all the rest: the willow leaves
Elysian-silvered, the grass so fully fledged

And unimprinted it can't not conjure thoughts
Of passing spirit-troops, *animae, quibus altera fato
Corpora debentur*, 'spirits,' that is,

'To whom second bodies are owed by fate'.
And now to continue, as enjoined to often,
'In my own words':

'All these presences
Once they have rolled time's wheel a thousand years
Are summoned here to drink the river water

[197]

So that memories of this underworld are shed
And soul is longing to dwell in flesh and blood
Under the dome of the sky.'

Route 110

for Anna Rose

I

In a stained front-buttoned shopcoat –
Sere brown piped with crimson –
Out of the Classics bay into an aisle

Smelling of dry rot and disinfectant
She emerges, absorbed in her coin-count,
Eyes front, right hand at work

In the slack marsupial vent
Of her change-pocket, thinking what to charge
For a used copy of *Aeneid* VI.

Dustbreath bestirred in the cubicle mouth
I inhaled as she slid my purchase
Into a deckle-edged brown paper bag.

Smithfield Market Saturdays. The pet shop
Fetid with droppings in the rabbit cages,
Melodious with canaries, green and gold,

But silent now as birdless Lake Avernus.
I hurried on, shortcutting to the buses,
Parrying the crush with my bagged Virgil,

Past booths and the jambs of booths with their displays
Of canvas schoolbags, maps, prints, plaster plaques,
Feather dusters, artificial flowers,

Then racks of suits and overcoats that swayed
When one was tugged from its overcrowded frame
Like their owners' shades close-packed on Charon's barge.

III

Once the driver wound a little handle
The destination names began to roll
Fast-forward in their panel, and everything

Came to life. Passengers
Flocked to the kerb like agitated rooks
Around a rookery, all go

But undecided. At which point the inspector
Who ruled the roost in bus station and bus
Separated and directed everybody

By calling not the names but the route numbers,
And so we scattered as instructed, me
For Route 110, Cookstown via Toome and Magherafelt.

Tarpaulin-stiff, coal-black, sharp-cuffed as slate,
The standard-issue railway guard's long coat
I bought once second-hand: suffering its scourge

At the neck and wrists was worth it even so
For the dismay I caused by doorstep night arrivals,
A creature of cold blasts and flap-winged rain.

And then, come finer weather, up and away
To Italy, in a wedding guest's bargain suit
Of finest weave, loose-fitting, summery, grey

As Venus' doves, hotfooting it with the tanned expats
Up their Etruscan slopes to a small brick chapel
To find myself the one there most at home.

V

Venus' doves? Why not McNicholls' pigeons
Out of their pigeon holes but homing still?
They lead unerringly to McNicholls' kitchen

And a votive jampot on the dresser shelf.
So reach me not a gentian but stalks
From the bunch that stood in it, each head of oats

A silvered smattering, each individual grain
Wrapped in a second husk of glittering foil
They'd saved from chocolate bars, then pinched
    and cinched

'To give the wee altar a bit of shine.'
The night old Mrs Nick, as she was to us,
Handed me one it as good as lit me home.

VI

It was the age of ghosts. Of hand-held flashlamps.
Lights moving at a distance scried for who
And why: whose wake, say, in which house on the road

In that direction – Michael Mulholland's the first
I attended as a full participant,
Sitting up until the family rose

Like strangers to themselves and us. A wake
Without the corpse of their own dear ill-advised
Sonbrother swimmer, lost in the Bristol Channel.

For three nights we kept conversation going
Around the waiting trestles. By the fourth
His coffin, with the lid on, was in place.

VII

The corpse house then a house of hospitalities
Right through the small hours, the ongoing card game
Interrupted constantly by rounds

Of cigarettes on plates, biscuits, cups of tea,
The antiphonal recital of known events
And others rare, clandestine, undertoned.

Apt pupil in their night school, I walked home
On the last morning, my clothes as smoke-imbued
As if I'd fed a pyre, accompanied to the gable

By the mother, to point out a right of way
Across their fields, into our own back lane,
And absolve me thus formally of trespass.

As one when the month is young sees a new moon
Fading into daytime, again it is her face
At the dormer window, her hurt still new,

My look behind me hurried as I unlock,
Switch on, rev up, pull out and drive away
In the car she'll not have taken her eyes off,

The brakelights flicker-flushing at the corner
Like red lamps swung by RUC patrols
In the small hours on pre-Troubles roads

After dances, after our holdings on
And holdings back, the necking
And nay-saying age of impurity.

And what in the end was there left to bury
Of Mr Lavery, blown up in his own pub
As he bore the primed device and bears it still

Mid-morning towards the sun-admitting door
Of Ashley House? Or of Louis O'Neill
In the wrong place the Wednesday they buried

Thirteen who'd been shot in Derry? Or of bodies
Unglorified, accounted for and bagged
Behind the grief cordons: not to be laid

In war graves with full honours, nor in a separate plot
Fired over on anniversaries
By units drilled and spruce and unreconciled.

X

Virgil's happy shades in pure blanched raiment
Contend on their green meadows, while Orpheus
Weaves among them, sweeping strings, aswerve

To the pulse of his own playing and to avoid
The wrestlers, dancers, runners on the grass.
Not unlike a sports day in Bellaghy,

Slim Whitman's wavering tenor amplified
Above sparking dodgems, flying chair-o-planes,
A mile of road with parked cars in the twilight

And teams of grown men stripped for action
Going hell for leather until the final whistle,
Leaving stud-scrapes on the pitch and on each other.

Those evenings when we'd just wait and watch
And fish. Then the evening the otter's head
Appeared in the flow, or was it only

A surface-ruck and gleam we took for
An otter's head? No doubting, all the same,
The gleam, a turnover warp in the black

Quick water. Or doubting the solid ground
Of the riverbank field, twilit and a-hover
With midge-drifts, as if we had commingled

Among shades and shadows stirring on the brink
And stood there waiting, watching,
Needy and ever needier for translation.

And now the age of births. As when once
At dawn from the foot of our back garden
The last to leave came with fresh-plucked flowers

To quell whatever smells of drink and smoke
Would linger on where mother and child were due
Later that morning from the nursing home,

So now, as a thank-offering for one
Whose long wait on the shaded bank has ended,
I arrive with my bunch of stalks and silvered heads

Like tapers that won't dim
As her earthlight breaks and we gather round
Talking baby talk.

Wraiths

for Ciaran Carson

I *Sidhe*

She took me into the ground, the spade-marked
Clean-cut inside of a dugout
Meant for calves.

Dung on the floor, a damp gleam
And seam of sand like white gold
In the earth wall, nicked fibres in the roof.

We stood under the hill, out of the day
But faced towards the daylight, holding hands,
Inhaling the excavated bank.

Zoom in over our shoulders,
A tunnelling shot that accelerates and flares.
Discover us against weird brightness. Cut.

ii *Parking Lot*

We were wraiths in the afternoon.
The bus had stopped. There was neither waiting room
Nor booth nor bench, only a parking lot

Above the town, open as a hillfort,
A panned sky and a light wind blowing.
We were on our way to the Gaeltacht,

Between languages, half in thrall to desire,
Half shy of it, when a flit of the foreknown
Blinked off a sunlit lake near the horizon

And passed into us, climbing and clunking up
Those fretted metal steps, as we reboarded
And were reincarnated seat by seat.

III *White Nights*

Furrow-plodders in spats and bright clasped brogues
Are cradling bags and hoisting beribboned drones
As their skilled neck-pullers' fingers force the chanters

And the whole band starts rehearsing
Its stupendous, swaggering march
Inside the hall. Meanwhile

One twilit field and summer hedge away
We wait for the learner who will stay behind
Piping by stops and starts,

Making an injured music for us alone,
Early-to-beds, white-night absentees
Open-eared to this day.

'The door was open and the house was dark'

in memory of David Hammond

The door was open and the house was dark
Wherefore I called his name, although I knew
The answer this time would be silence

That kept me standing listening while it grew
Backwards and down and out into the street
Where as I'd entered (I remember now)

The streetlamps too were out.
I felt, for the first time there and then, a stranger,
Intruder almost, wanting to take flight

Yet well aware that here there was no danger,
Only withdrawal, a not unwelcoming
Emptiness, as in a midnight hangar

On an overgrown airfield in late summer.

In the Attic

I

Like Jim Hawkins aloft in the cross-trees
Of *Hispaniola,* nothing underneath him
But still green water and clean bottom sand,

The ship aground, the canted mast far out
Above a sea-floor where striped fish pass in shoals –
And when they've passed, the face of Israel Hands

That rose in the shrouds before Jim shot him dead
Appears to rise again . . . 'But he was dead enough,'
The story says, 'being both shot and drowned.'

II

A birch tree planted twenty years ago
Comes between the Irish Sea and me
At the attic skylight, a man marooned

In his own loft, a boy
Shipshaped in the crow's nest of a life,
Airbrushed to and fro, wind-drunk, braced

By all that's thrumming up from keel to masthead,
Rubbing his eyes to believe them and this most
Buoyant, billowy, topgallant birch.

III

Ghost-footing what was then the *terra firma*
Of hallway linoleum, grandfather now appears,
His voice a-waver like the draught-prone screen

They'd set up in the Club Rooms earlier
For the matinee I've just come back from.
'And Isaac Hands,' he asks, 'Was Isaac in it?'

His memory of the name a-waver too,
His mistake perpetual, once and for all,
Like the single splash when Israel's body fell.

IV

As I age and blank on names,
As my uncertainty on stairs
Is more and more the lightheadedness

Of a cabin boy's first time on the rigging,
As the memorable bottoms out
Into the irretrievable,

It's not that I can't imagine still
That slight untoward rupture and world-tilt
As a wind freshened and the anchor weighed.

A Kite for Aibhín

after 'L'Aquilone' by Giovanni Pascoli (1855–1912)

Air from another life and time and place,
Pale blue heavenly air is supporting
A white wing beating high against the breeze,

And yes, it is a kite! As when one afternoon
All of us there trooped out
Among the briar hedges and stripped thorn,

I take my stand again, halt opposite
Anahorish Hill to scan the blue,
Back in that field to launch our long-tailed comet.

And now it hovers, tugs, veers, dives askew,
Lifts itself, goes with the wind until
It rises to loud cheers from us below.

Rises, and my hand is like a spindle
Unspooling, the kite a thin-stemmed flower
Climbing and carrying, carrying farther, higher

The longing in the breast and planted feet
And gazing face and heart of the kite flier
Until string breaks and – separate, elate –

The kite takes off, itself alone, a windfall.

In Time

for Síofra

Energy, balance, outbreak:
Listening to Bach
I saw you years from now
(More years than I'll be allowed)
Your toddler wobbles gone,
A sure and grown woman.

Your bare foot on the floor
Keeps me in step; the power
I first felt come up through
Our cement floor long ago
Palps your sole and heel
And earths you here for real.

An oratorio
Would be just the thing for you:
Energy, balance, outbreak
At play for their own sake
But for now we foot it lightly
In time, and silently.

18 August 2013

Index